CHRISTMAS CACTUS FOR BEGINNERS

*The Complete Indoor Plant Care Guide To Growing,
Blooming, And Propagating Schlumbergera With
Stunning Holiday Flowers And Year-Round Beauty*

LOVETT G. LAURIE

Disclaimer

This book is intended for educational and informational purposes only. While every effort has been made to ensure the accuracy of the information provided, the author and publisher make no guarantees regarding specific results. Plant growth and health depend on various factors including environment, care practices, and individual conditions.

The advice and techniques in this book reflect general best practices for Christmas cactus care, but may need to be adapted based on your local climate or plant variety. Always consult a local gardening expert or horticulturist for specific concerns.

INTRODUCTION
The Christmas Cactus

The Christmas Cactus has enchanted generations of plant lovers with its pendulous blooms, striking segmented stems, and a near-magical ability to flower during the most festive time of the year. Often gifted during the holidays and lovingly passed down as houseplant heirlooms, this plant belongs to the *Schlumbergera* genus—tropical cacti that defy the typical desert-dwelling image most associate with the cactus family.

What is a Christmas Cactus?

The Christmas Cactus is a **tropical epiphytic plant** from the genus *Schlumbergera*, native to the cloud forests of southeastern Brazil. Unlike the typical cactus that thrives in arid deserts, this species lives in humid, shaded, high-altitude rainforests, often perched on trees or rock crevices. Rather than relying on thick spines or waxy skins to conserve water, it absorbs moisture and nutrients from decaying organic matter around it.

Botanically known as *Schlumbergera x buckleyi*, the Christmas Cactus is a **hybrid species** that originated from the crossbreeding of other *Schlumbergera* species in cultivation. This hybrid is characterized by its flattened stem segments (technically called cladodes), gracefully arching growth habit, and vibrant tubular flowers that bloom primarily in late December in the Northern Hemisphere—hence its common name.

6

While commonly referred to as a cactus, the Christmas Cactus differs markedly in care requirements and appearance. It needs **higher humidity, regular watering, and filtered light**, making it more akin to a tropical houseplant than a typical desert succulent.

A few key characteristics of the Christmas Cactus include:

- **Segmented, leaf-like stems** that feel fleshy but not spiny
- **Bright, pendulous blooms** in pink, red, white, yellow, or purple shades
- **Day-length sensitivity** that triggers blooming in winter (short days, long nights)
- **Long lifespan**, often living for decades when properly cared for
- **Non-toxic foliage**, making it safe around pets and children

Its seasonal bloom time, unusual for most houseplants, makes it a popular fixture in holiday decor and gifting.

History and Origins of Schlumbergera

The history of the Christmas Cactus is a fascinating journey from **tropical mountaintops to windowsills around the world**. The *Schlumbergera* genus was first documented in the early 19th century during botanical explorations of Brazil's coastal cloud forests.

Native Habitat

In the high-altitude forests of southeastern Brazil—especially in the coastal mountain ranges such as the Serra do Mar—plants in the *Schlumbergera* genus grow

7

epiphytically, meaning they live on other plants (mostly trees) without parasitizing them. They receive filtered sunlight and enjoy the constant moisture from rain and cloud condensation. These natural conditions are vastly different from what we think of when we hear "cactus," which has led to some confusion among plant owners and retailers.

Discovery and Classification
The first species of this genus were introduced to Europe in the 1810s and 1820s by plant collectors who brought specimens back from Brazil. One of the most significant figures in the classification of this plant was **Frederic Schlumberger**, a French collector and cultivator, for whom the genus was eventually named.

Development of the Christmas Cactus
In the mid-19th century, horticulturists in Europe began crossbreeding species such as *Schlumbergera truncata* and *Schlumbergera russelliana*. The result of this cross was *Schlumbergera x buckleyi*—what we now call the Christmas Cactus. It was named after **William Buckley,** the chief gardener at the Rollisson Nurseries in England, who first developed the hybrid around 1850.

This hybrid was particularly popular due to its reliable winter blooming cycle, which coincided with Christmas. Over time, breeders refined its bloom colors and growth habits, leading to the wide variety of cultivars we have today.

Commercial Growth and Popularity

The Christmas Cactus gained commercial popularity in the 20th century, especially in North America and Europe. It became one of the most common holiday houseplants sold in garden centers and supermarkets during November and December.

Why It's Loved: Holiday Blooms and Easy Care

Few houseplants are as well-timed, meaningful, and **low-maintenance** as the Christmas Cactus. It has earned its place as a cherished home companion for several compelling reasons.

Seasonal Significance

The most celebrated feature of the Christmas Cactus is its ability to bloom just as winter settles in. With its radiant flowers emerging in December, it becomes a symbol of **hope, celebration, and renewal**—qualities deeply tied to the holiday season. For many, the blooming of a Christmas Cactus becomes an annual family event, as it often coincides with holiday decorations going up.

Ease of Propagation and Sharing

Another reason it is adored is its **ease of propagation**. A single stem segment can root and grow into a new plant, making it one of the most shared houseplants across generations. It's not uncommon for people to own a plant that originated from a cutting decades old—sometimes over 50 or even 100 years. This ease of sharing has made the Christmas Cactus a **symbol of**

connection, memory, and continuity within families and communities.

Low Maintenance, High Reward

Though it requires more water and humidity than its desert cousins, the Christmas Cactus is **incredibly adaptable and forgiving** when placed in the right environment. When basic needs are met—such as indirect light, moderate watering, and a cool period before blooming—it thrives with little fuss. Unlike some high-maintenance tropical houseplants, it tolerates a bit of neglect and often surprises its owners with brilliant flowers even after less-than-ideal conditions.

Air Purifying and Safe for Pets

In addition to being aesthetically pleasing, the Christmas Cactus is **non-toxic to cats and dogs** and has some air-purifying qualities. This makes it a safe and wholesome addition to homes with children or pets, increasing its appeal among families.

Common Names and Misconceptions

The Christmas Cactus is often confused with other closely related species in the *Schlumbergera* genus, and even sold under incorrect names. These errors have led to widespread misconceptions in plant identification, care, and bloom timing.

Alternate Common Names

- Holiday Cactus

- Crab Cactus (refers to the claw-like shape of some segment edges)
- Thanksgiving Cactus
- Easter Cactus
- Schlumbergera
- Zygocactus (older but outdated term)

While "Holiday Cactus" is sometimes used as a catch-all term, it actually refers to **three different species or hybrids** with similar appearances but distinct blooming periods and physical characteristics.

Misidentification in Stores

A common issue arises with mass-produced plants sold around the holidays. Most plants labeled "Christmas Cactus" in stores are **actually Thanksgiving Cactus** (*Schlumbergera truncata*) due to its earlier bloom time (November) and easier cultivation in greenhouse conditions. True Christmas Cactus (*S. x buckleyi*) blooms later, often closer to late December or early January.

The confusion between these species is largely due to **visual similarity and commercial mislabeling**. Without understanding the subtle differences in the stem edges and flower structure, most consumers never realize they own a different species than the one they intended to buy.

Christmas Cactus vs. Thanksgiving and Easter Cactus

Understanding the distinctions between the **three primary "holiday cacti"**—Christmas Cactus, Thanksgiving Cactus, and Easter Cactus—is essential for proper care, identification, and bloom expectation. Though they all belong to the cactus family and the *Schlumbergera* or closely related *Hatiora* genus, each has unique traits.

1. Christmas Cactus (*Schlumbergera x buckleyi*)

- **Stem shape:** Rounded, scalloped edges
- **Bloom time:** Late December to January
- **Flowers:** Symmetrical, hanging downward, usually with soft curves
- **Growth habit:** More pendulous, graceful arching stems
- **Color:** Available in red, white, pink, and purple varieties
- **Hybrid origin:** Cross between *S. russelliana* and *S. truncata*

2. Thanksgiving Cactus (*Schlumbergera truncata*)

- **Stem shape:** Pointed, toothed segments with sharp edges (like crab claws)
- **Bloom time:** Mid to late November
- **Flowers:** More upright, zygomorphic (bilaterally symmetrical), typically with more vibrant, angular form
- **Growth habit:** More upright and bushy compared to the Christmas Cactus

12

- **Color:** Wide range, including orange, peach, and magenta
- **Often mislabeled as:** Christmas Cactus in garden centers

3. Easter Cactus (*Hatiora gaertneri* or *Rhipsalidopsis gaertneri*)

- **Stem shape:** Rounded with slight notches
- **Bloom time:** March to May
- **Flowers:** Star-shaped and symmetrical
- **Growth habit:** Upright to semi-arching
- **Color:** Often bright pink, red, or lavender
- **Genus:** Not a *Schlumbergera*, but closely related and has similar care needs

Key Takeaway:
If your cactus is blooming in **November** with pointed leaves, you likely have a Thanksgiving Cactus. If it blooms in **December** and has smooth, scalloped edges, it's a true Christmas Cactus. Blooms around **springtime** suggest an Easter Cactus.

This distinction is not merely academic—it impacts **bloom timing, temperature requirements, dormancy cycles, and pruning schedules**. Knowing exactly which type of cactus you have empowers you to provide the ideal care conditions for consistent yearly blooms.

In conclusion, the Christmas Cactus is far more than a decorative houseplant. It's a resilient, long-living botanical companion with rich historical roots, cherished cultural significance, and a delightful bloom

13

cycle that brings joy during the darkest part of the year. As you begin your journey with this plant, understanding its true nature—beyond the labels and myths—will prepare you to nurture it with care, and perhaps even pass it on as a living legacy.

CHAPTER ONE

UNDERSTANDING THE CHRISTMAS CACTUS FAMILY

The Christmas Cactus is often admired for its vibrant blooms and surprising winter flowering season, but behind its popularity lies a fascinating botanical lineage and a set of unique growth characteristics that set it apart from other houseplants and even from its desert-dwelling cactus cousins. Understanding the biological family and traits of this plant not only clarifies common confusions around its care and identification but also deepens one's appreciation of its evolutionary design and botanical beauty.

This chapter offers an in-depth look into the **botanical classification, key traits, growth habits, bloom varieties**, and the specifics of how to confidently identify a true Christmas Cactus among similar species.

Botanical Classification and Species Overview

The plant known as the Christmas Cactus belongs to the **family Cactaceae**, which encompasses all true cacti. However, unlike many members of this family, which are adapted to hot, arid environments, the Christmas Cactus is a **tropical epiphyte** that hails from the humid cloud forests of southeastern Brazil. Within Cactaceae, the Christmas Cactus is a member of the **tribe Rhipsalideae**, a group characterized by epiphytic habits and spineless stems.

The **botanical name** of the traditional Christmas Cactus is *Schlumbergera* × *buckleyi*, a **hybrid** created through the cross-pollination of two parent species:

- *Schlumbergera truncata* (often called the Thanksgiving Cactus)
- *Schlumbergera russelliana* (a species native to the moist forests of Brazil)

This hybridization was first achieved in the 19th century by horticulturists aiming to create a plant that bloomed during the winter holiday season. Since then, many cultivars and hybrids have been developed, leading to a wide variety of Christmas Cactus forms and colors.

The **Schlumbergera genus** currently contains about **6 recognized species**, and each has played a role in the development of modern-day holiday cacti. Here's a brief overview of the most relevant species:

- **Schlumbergera truncata**: Sometimes mislabeled as Christmas Cactus; blooms in late fall; sharp, claw-like stem edges.
- **Schlumbergera russelliana**: One of the parents of the Christmas Cactus hybrid; rounded stem edges, trailing habit.
- **Schlumbergera × buckleyi**: The true Christmas Cactus; hybrid of *S. truncata* and *S. russelliana*.

- **Schlumbergera orssichiana** and **Schlumbergera opuntioides**: Less common in home cultivation but used in breeding programs to introduce new flower shapes and growth habits.
- **Hatiora gaertneri** (formerly part of *Schlumbergera*): Commonly known as the Easter Cactus; blooms in spring, with star-shaped flowers.

These species and their hybrids differ in stem shape, bloom time, and floral symmetry, yet they share many key characteristics, particularly in how they grow and reproduce.

Key Traits: Flattened Stems, No Thorns

One of the most defining features of the Christmas Cactus and its relatives is the **flattened, segmented stems**. These are technically known as **cladodes**—flattened leaf-like stem segments that perform photosynthesis in place of true leaves, which the plant lacks.

Unlike typical desert cacti that possess sharp spines or thick, round stems to conserve water, Christmas Cactus plants have evolved to fit a very different ecological niche. In their natural habitat, nestled in the forks of tree branches or on moss-covered rocks, these plants receive ample moisture and filtered light. Their structure reflects this adaptation:

- **Segmented Stems**: The cladodes are joined end-to-end, with each segment resembling a notched or scalloped paddle.
- **Absence of Thorns**: True Christmas Cactus plants lack the defensive spines associated with many cacti.

17

They may have very tiny bristles at the areoles (stem joints), but these are soft and non-injurious.

- **Smooth, Glossy Texture**: The cladodes have a somewhat waxy or glossy surface, helping to retain moisture in a high-humidity environment.
- **Non-Succulent Appearance**: While they do store water, their stems do not appear thick or succulent in the way that desert cacti do.

These physical adaptations allow the plant to thrive in the canopy environment of the rainforest, where soil is scarce but light and organic debris are plentiful.

Additionally, these segments allow for easy propagation. A single segment or cutting containing several joints can readily develop roots in moist conditions, making the Christmas Cactus one of the easiest houseplants to share and multiply.

Growth Habits: Epiphyte Behavior

One of the most misunderstood aspects of the Christmas Cactus family is their **epiphytic** nature. The term "epiphyte" refers to a plant that grows upon another plant—usually a tree—without drawing nutrients from it. In other words, epiphytes are not parasitic. They simply use the host tree as a structure to reach better light and airflow.

In the wild, Christmas Cactus species grow along **tree trunks and branches** in Brazil's coastal rainforests. Here's how this unique behavior influences its structure and care:

18

- **Root System**: Epiphytes have shallow, fine roots that anchor them into crevices filled with leaf litter, moss, or other organic matter. As such, they do not need deep pots or heavy soil in cultivation.
- **Humidity Needs**: Because they evolved in moist environments, these cacti require more humidity than most desert succulents. Dry air can lead to shriveled segments or failed blooming.
- **Filtered Light**: The forest canopy protects them from direct sun. They thrive under filtered or diffused light rather than full, intense exposure. Indoors, a bright window with indirect light is ideal.
- **Trailing Habit**: Their natural form is **pendulous or cascading**, allowing them to drape beautifully over tree branches—or, in homes, over the sides of hanging baskets and elevated pots.

These growth habits also contribute to their popularity as ornamental plants. Their **weeping shape**, combined with vivid flowers, makes them excellent candidates for hanging displays or tall plant stands.

Understanding their epiphytic background helps gardeners avoid common mistakes, such as overwatering (due to poor drainage) or placing them in full sun, which can lead to sunburn or stress.

Color Variants and Bloom Shapes

One of the reasons the Christmas Cactus has remained so popular for generations is its **stunning array of flower colors and shapes**. Modern breeding has expanded the original color palette significantly, offering a diverse

19

range of visual styles to suit any decor or personal preference.

Natural Flower Structure

The classic bloom of the Christmas Cactus is **tubular**, with petals that flare outwards in a graceful, layered arrangement. The flowers emerge from the joints (areoles) at the tips of the stem segments and are often **pendulous**, meaning they hang downwards. This drooping habit enhances their beauty, especially in hanging arrangements.

The flower consists of **multiple whorls of petals**, often giving the appearance of a double-layered blossom. Long **stamens** protrude from the center, tipped with bright pollen and often adding contrast to the bloom color.

Color Variants

While the original hybrids primarily bloomed in shades of red and magenta, today's Christmas Cactus cultivars include:

- **Crimson red**
- **Soft pink**
- **Fuchsia**
- **Bright white**
- **Lavender or purple**
- **Peach or salmon**
- **Yellow or golden tones** (less common but increasingly available)

These colors are the result of **selective hybridization**, with breeders using various *Schlumbergera* species to introduce new hues and patterns. Some cultivars also feature **bicolor blooms**, where the base of the flower is one color and the tips another, creating a dramatic visual effect.

Bloom Triggers

It's important to note that flower production in Christmas Cactus is highly sensitive to **photoperiod and temperature**. Flower buds form when the plant experiences:

- **Short day length**: Approximately 12–14 hours of uninterrupted darkness per day for 4–6 weeks
- **Cooler temperatures**: Around 50–60°F (10–15°C)

This sensitivity to seasonal changes is what triggers blooming in late fall and winter, aligning naturally with the holiday season.

How to Identify Authentic Christmas Cactus

Due to overlapping characteristics among holiday cacti and widespread mislabeling by retailers, it can be difficult for even experienced gardeners to distinguish a true Christmas Cactus (*Schlumbergera* × *buckleyi*) from similar species like the Thanksgiving Cactus (*S. truncata*) or Easter Cactus (*Hatiora gaertneri*). However, several distinct features can help identify the authentic plant.

1. Stem Segment Shape

This is one of the most reliable indicators:

- **Christmas Cactus**: Rounded or scalloped segment edges with no sharp points. The edges are smooth and softly curved.
- **Thanksgiving Cactus**: Prominent pointed "teeth" along the segment edges; resembles crab claws.
- **Easter Cactus**: Segment edges are more oval and symmetrical, with shallow notches.

2. Flower Orientation and Shape

- **Christmas Cactus**: Flowers are more symmetrical and **hang downward**.
- **Thanksgiving Cactus**: Flowers are **more angular** and may grow horizontally or upright.
- **Easter Cactus**: Blooms are **star-shaped** and emerge in spring.

3. Bloom Timing
While indoor conditions can sometimes shift bloom timing, the natural tendencies are:

- **Christmas Cactus**: Blooms **late December to January**
- **Thanksgiving Cactus**: Blooms **mid to late November**
- **Easter Cactus**: Blooms **March to May**

4. Growth Habit

- **Christmas Cactus**: Trailing and pendulous. Ideal for hanging baskets.
- **Thanksgiving Cactus**: More upright and branching.
- **Easter Cactus**: Compact, with thicker, stiffer segments.

22

5. Areole Position

The points from which flowers and roots grow (areoles) are slightly sunken and not very prominent on the Christmas Cactus compared to the others.

Practical Identification Tip

If your "Christmas Cactus" is blooming before Thanksgiving and has sharply pointed segments, it is most likely a Thanksgiving Cactus mislabeled for seasonal sales. Authentic Christmas Cactus typically begins blooming closer to the **actual Christmas period**, with softer, trailing features.

Embracing the Christmas Cactus for What It Is

Understanding the full botanical background and traits of the Christmas Cactus transforms your experience as a grower. Rather than simply treating it as a seasonal decoration, recognizing its identity as an epiphytic, tropical cactus with a long hybrid history allows you to care for it with precision and purpose.

From its segmented, spineless stems to its colorful, winter blooms, the Christmas Cactus embodies the **diversity of the cactus family** and the magic of plant evolution. With correct identification and an appreciation for its unique characteristics, you can ensure your plant thrives—and perhaps even becomes a treasured heirloom passed down for generations.

CHOOSING THE RIGHT PLANT

When it comes to cultivating a beautiful, long-living Christmas Cactus, the journey begins with choosing the right plant. Whether you're purchasing your first plant from a nursery or receiving one as a heartfelt gift, starting with a healthy, well-cared-for specimen is the foundation of successful growth and blooming.

Where to Buy Healthy Plants

Knowing where to source a healthy Christmas Cactus is the first—and arguably most critical—step in your plant care journey. Not all sellers offer the same quality, and choosing a substandard plant can lead to disappointment, stress, or unexpected challenges that are avoidable with a little knowledge.

Local Nurseries and Garden Centers

Brick-and-mortar garden centers and locally owned nurseries often offer the healthiest and most reliable stock. These plants are usually grown on-site or sourced from reputable growers who specialize in *Schlumbergera* hybrids. One major advantage is that these establishments typically provide:

- Proper care prior to purchase (adequate light, watering, pest control)
- Staff knowledgeable about plant needs and species
- Accurate labeling (helpful in identifying true Christmas Cactus vs. Thanksgiving Cactus)
- Healthier root systems due to consistent care and monitoring

Big Box Stores and Supermarkets

Many large chain retailers and grocery stores stock Christmas Cactus plants during the holiday season. While convenient, plants from these locations often suffer from rushed production and poor handling. Common issues include:

- Overwatering or underwatering in-store
- Incorrect labeling (many are actually Thanksgiving Cactus sold as "Christmas Cactus")
- Damaged stems or roots from bulk transport
- Potted in dense, moisture-retaining soil not suitable for epiphytic plants

If you choose to buy from a big box retailer, it's important to **inspect the plant thoroughly** and be prepared to repot or rehabilitate it soon after purchase.

Online Plant Retailers

The rise of e-commerce has made buying plants online more popular than ever. Reputable online nurseries can provide access to rare varieties and colors not available locally. However, this route requires more diligence:

- Choose sellers with clear shipping policies and plant guarantees
- Look for photos of the **actual plant** you'll receive, not just stock images
- Consider shipping delays and how they may affect the plant's health
- Make sure the plant is shipped in protective packaging to avoid breakage

Online plant shopping is best for intermediate growers who can quickly identify and recover from any transplant shock the plant may experience during shipping.

Plant Swaps and Social Gifting

Many Christmas Cactus enthusiasts receive their plants through **cuttings or swaps with friends and family**. This is a time-honored tradition, and many thriving plants in homes today are decades old, passed down through generations. While this is a heartwarming way to acquire a plant, ensure:

- The donor plant is healthy, free of pests or rot
- The cutting has at least **2–3 segments** for optimal rooting
- You receive proper care instructions if you're new to propagation

Signs of a Thriving Cactus

Whether you're evaluating a plant at a nursery or just received one as a gift, being able to identify the signs of health will set you up for success. A thriving Christmas Cactus exhibits a combination of external and internal vitality.

1. Firm, Glossy Stem Segments

Healthy Christmas Cactus segments (cladodes) should feel firm, slightly flexible, and have a **rich green or slightly purplish hue** depending on light exposure. The surface should be free from blemishes, wrinkles, or rot.

Avoid plants with:

- Wilted or drooping segments
- Wrinkled stems (a sign of dehydration or root problems)
- Yellowing or soft tissue (could signal overwatering or fungal issues)

2. Even, Upright Growth

A well-structured Christmas Cactus will have an **upright to gently arching shape,** with segments growing in a balanced pattern. Lopsided growth may indicate insufficient light or prior damage. While asymmetry alone is not a dealbreaker, it may signal that the plant has not been rotated regularly or has grown under suboptimal conditions.

3. Evidence of New Growth

New segments forming at the tips or visible flower buds are excellent signs. New growth is usually:

- Lighter green or slightly reddish at the tips
- Firm to the touch
- Free of visible pests or scarring

4. Intact Root System (if visible)

If you're able to gently lift the plant from its pot (with permission, if in-store), look for:

- White or light tan roots that are firm and branching
- A root ball that is not overly compacted
- Moisture that feels slightly damp, but not soaked

5. Active Bloom or Bud Development

In the holiday season, a healthy plant may already have buds or flowers. Blooms should:

- Emerge from the joints between segments
- Appear vibrant, symmetrical, and free from fungal spots
- Not be dropping prematurely (which can indicate stress or recent relocation)

Selecting Based on Bloom Color

One of the most delightful aspects of owning a Christmas Cactus is its spectacular blooms. Modern cultivars come in a **wide range of colors,** allowing you to choose based on personal taste, holiday décor, or symbolic meaning.

Common Color Varieties

- **Crimson Red**: Traditional and festive; often associated with warmth and passion.
- **Snow White**: Clean and elegant; pairs well with winter-themed decor.
- **Fuchsia or Magenta**: Bright and bold; excellent for lively rooms or modern interiors.
- **Peach or Salmon**: Softer tones ideal for neutral palettes or subtle accenting.
- **Lavender or Purple**: Unique and mystical; a favorite for collectors and exotic plant lovers.
- **Yellow or Gold**: Rare and increasingly popular; symbolizes cheer and prosperity.

Each bloom color may vary slightly depending on light exposure and genetics. Some hybrids may even produce **two-tone or gradient blossoms**, blending pink into white or orange into red.

How to Choose the Right Color for You

- **For Holiday Matching**: Red and white are most traditional and pair well with classic Christmas themes.
- **For Year-Round Display**: Softer shades like peach or lavender work well beyond the holidays.
- **For Collectors**: Seek rare cultivars or dual-color varieties. These are often found online or at specialty nurseries.

Be cautious with plants **not yet in bloom**—they may be labeled with a bloom color that doesn't match what will eventually emerge. Purchasing during the blooming period ensures you get exactly the color you desire.

Inspecting for Pests and Diseases

A thorough inspection before purchase is crucial. Even a healthy-looking plant can harbor pests or fungal pathogens that take time to emerge. Early detection saves time, money, and the risk of spreading problems to other houseplants.

Common Pests to Watch For

1. **Mealybugs**

- Appear as small, cottony clumps near stem joints
- Feed on sap, leading to shriveled segments

29

- Can spread rapidly to nearby houseplants

2. **Fungus Gnats**

- Small black flies that hover around the soil
- Indicate overwatering and decaying organic matter
- Larvae can damage roots

3. **Spider Mites**

- Tiny, often invisible to the naked eye
- Create fine webbing between segments
- Cause stippling or pale dots on leaves

4. **Scale Insects**

- Brown or white bump-like insects attached to stems
- Difficult to remove once established
- Cause yellowing and stunted growth

Early Signs of Disease

1. **Root Rot**

- Caused by overwatering or dense, poorly draining soil
- Roots appear dark brown, mushy, or smell foul
- Stems may sag or blacken near the soil line

2. **Stem Rot**

- Black or brown lesions at the base of the segments
- Can spread rapidly upward if not treated
- Requires immediate pruning and isolation

3. **Botrytis or Powdery Mildew**

- Fuzzy gray or white mold on stems or flowers
- Associated with poor air circulation or high humidity
- Remove affected areas and reduce moisture levels

Inspection Tips

- Check both top and bottom sides of segments
- Look closely at joints where pests hide
- Gently disturb the soil and observe for gnat activity
- Smell the plant—foul or musty odors may indicate rot

If pests are present but minor, you may still consider purchasing if you're confident in your ability to quarantine and treat the plant. However, for beginners, it's advisable to choose a plant free from any visible signs of trouble.

Gifting and Receiving Christmas Cactus

One of the most charming traditions associated with the Christmas Cactus is its frequent use as a **living holiday gift**. Its blooms symbolize warmth, love, and resilience—making it a meaningful, long-lasting alternative to cut flowers or disposable decorations.

Why It Makes a Perfect Gift

- **Symbol of Long Life and Renewal**: With proper care, a Christmas Cactus can live for decades, blooming faithfully every year.
- **Non-Toxic**: Safe for households with pets or children.
- **Easy to Maintain**: Once acclimated, these plants require minimal attention.

31

- **Sentimental Value**: Ideal for passing down between generations or gifting during significant milestones.

Best Practices When Gifting

1. **Choose a Blooming Plant**
   A flowering plant feels more festive and gives the recipient instant gratification. Wrap it in a decorative pot cover or ribbon for a seasonal touch.
2. **Include a Care Card**
   Most recipients will appreciate a simple care guide that outlines:

- Watering frequency
- Lighting needs
- Bloom care tips
- How to repot when necessary

3. **Transport Carefully**
   In colder climates, protect the plant from wind chill or frost during transit. Place it in a cardboard box or insulated bag for the ride home.
4. **Add a Personal Touch**
   Consider including a hand-written note, holiday ornament, or even a packet of fertilizer or cactus soil as part of the gift.

Receiving a Plant as a Gift

If you've received a Christmas Cactus:

- Let it acclimate for a few days before repotting or moving to a new location.

32

- Check for early signs of rot or pests from transport shock.
- Water sparingly, especially if it was recently watered before delivery.
- Observe the bloom time to help identify the specific hybrid.

Selecting the right Christmas Cactus is both an art and a science. It involves knowing where to shop, understanding what a healthy plant looks like, aligning color choices with your taste or seasonal themes, and carefully checking for pests and disease before bringing it into your home or gifting it to someone special.

Choosing wisely from the start sets the stage for years of low-maintenance beauty, dependable holiday blooms, and joyful connection. Whether your plant is bought, gifted, or inherited, a little attention during the selection process ensures you begin your journey with strength, resilience, and the promise of color when you need it most.

Would you like the next section to cover **Lighting and Temperature Needs, Repotting and Soil Preferences**, or move into **Holiday Bloom Cycles and How to Trigger Them?**

IDEAL INDOOR GROWING CONDITIONS

Creating the right indoor environment is essential for the success of the Christmas Cactus (*Schlumbergera* × *buckleyi*). Despite belonging to the cactus family, it defies the expectations most people have of cacti—it does not thrive in high heat, blazing sunlight, or dry air. Instead, it flourishes in conditions that mimic the **cool, humid, shaded cloud forests** of its native Brazil.

Understanding the specific needs of this plant in an indoor setting helps ensure not just survival, but **thriving growth, vibrant flowers, and long life**. This chapter breaks down the key environmental factors: temperature, humidity, lighting, air movement, and seasonal rhythms. These insights form the foundation of proper care and will empower both beginner and experienced growers to get the best performance from their Christmas Cactus year after year.

Temperature and Humidity Preferences

Temperature and humidity are two of the most misunderstood components in growing a healthy Christmas Cactus indoors. Unlike desert cacti, which enjoy hot and dry conditions, Christmas Cactus plants require **moderate temperatures and consistently high humidity** to simulate the conditions of their native epiphytic environment.

34

Optimal Temperature Range

Christmas Cactus thrives best in a temperature range of **60°F to 70°F (15°C to 21°C)** during the daytime and can tolerate nighttime drops to **50°F (10°C)**. These moderate conditions align with their natural tropical montane climate.

- **Ideal daytime range**: 65°F to 70°F (18°C to 21°C)
- **Ideal nighttime range**: 55°F to 60°F (13°C to 15°C)

Temperatures above **80°F (27°C)** can stress the plant, especially when combined with low humidity or excessive sunlight. Similarly, temperatures consistently below 50°F (10°C) can slow growth and may cause bud drop if the plant is actively developing flowers.

What to Avoid

- **Sudden temperature fluctuations**: Plants placed near drafty windows or heating vents may suffer from shock.
- **Heat stress**: Avoid direct placement near stoves, radiators, or sunny, unventilated windows.
- **Cold drafts**: During winter months, make sure plants near windows or doors are not exposed to freezing air leaks.

Humidity Requirements

Native to rainforests, Christmas Cactus requires a **humidity level of 50% to 60%** for optimal health. This is higher than the average indoor humidity in most homes, especially in winter when heating systems run.

Indicators of Low Humidity

- Dry, brittle stem segments
- Browning or yellowing tips
- Flower buds dropping prematurely
- General wilting or limpness despite watering

Ways to Increase Humidity Indoors

- **Humidity trays**: Place a shallow tray filled with water and pebbles under the plant's pot. As water evaporates, it adds moisture to the surrounding air.
- **Room humidifiers**: Use a humidifier in the plant room, especially during the heating season.
- **Grouping plants together**: Multiple plants transpiring in close proximity raise localized humidity.
- **Bathroom placement**: If lighting allows, bathrooms can be ideal due to their naturally humid environment.

Balancing temperature and humidity is critical. A humid environment with cool-to-moderate temperatures promotes stronger growth, better hydration, and resilient flowering.

Best Light Exposure for Blooming

Light is another essential factor in cultivating a successful Christmas Cactus, but unlike desert plants, this cactus does not require intense, direct sunlight. Instead, it prefers **bright but indirect light**, similar to the dappled light it would receive under a forest canopy.

Daily Light Requirements

- **6 to 8 hours** of bright, indirect sunlight per day is ideal.
- **Filtered light** through sheer curtains or blinds works well.
- Avoid placing the plant in total shade, which can cause poor growth and no flowering.

Ideal Indoor Locations

- **East-facing window**: Receives gentle morning sun; ideal for promoting healthy growth without scorching.
- **North-facing window**: May be adequate if it receives strong ambient light.
- **South or west-facing windows**: These can be used if filtered by a curtain to prevent direct afternoon sun, which can cause sunburn.

Signs of Improper Lighting

- **Too little light**:
  o Leggy or stretched-out growth
  o Poor flower production
  o Dull, dark green stems
- **Too much light**:
  o Yellow or reddish tinge on segments (a stress response)
  o Scorched or faded tissue
  o Flower buds dropping before opening

Bloom Initiation and Light Timing

For a Christmas Cactus to bloom reliably, it must experience **short-day conditions**, meaning fewer than 12 hours of light per day for a period of 4 to 6 weeks.

This photoperiod sensitivity is part of what triggers flowering.

Tips for promoting blooming through light control:

- In late September or early October, reduce light exposure gradually.
- Ensure the plant experiences **uninterrupted darkness** for 12–14 hours each night (avoid room lights or nearby lamps during this period).
- Move the plant away from artificial light sources or cover it with a light-blocking box or cloth each evening.

Providing the right light at the right time is one of the most influential factors in achieving a strong, consistent bloom.

Air Circulation and Room Placement

Proper air circulation is often overlooked in indoor gardening, but it plays a critical role in preventing fungal infections, rot, and pests. For Christmas Cactus, which thrives in moist environments, air movement helps balance humidity and keeps leaves and stems dry enough to avoid fungal issues.

The Role of Air Circulation

- Prevents **mildew and mold** from forming on stems or soil
- Discourages **fungus gnats and other pests**
- Enhances **transpiration**, improving overall plant health

- Supports even **temperature and humidity** distribution around the plant

Do's and Don'ts for Room Placement

- **Do** place the plant where it gets good airflow but is shielded from strong drafts.
- **Do** use a gentle fan if the room is stagnant or overly humid.
- **Don't** place it directly in front of heaters, air conditioners, or vents—this can dry the plant too quickly or create harmful temperature fluctuations.

Best Rooms for Christmas Cactus

- **Living rooms**: Often have large windows and consistent climate.
- **Bright kitchens**: Offer humidity and warmth but avoid proximity to stoves.
- **Bathrooms**: High humidity and warm temperatures are ideal, provided there's sufficient light.
- **Bedrooms or home offices**: Suitable as long as lighting and airflow are adequate.

A good rule of thumb: if you feel comfortable in the room, your Christmas Cactus probably will too—provided it has the right balance of light and moisture.

Seasonal Adjustments for Indoor Care

Christmas Cactus care is not static. As seasons change, so must your approach. This plant has distinct **seasonal needs** that align with its natural growth cycle: active growth in spring and summer, bloom preparation in fall, and flowering and rest in winter.

Spring and Summer: Growth Period

- Increase watering as days warm and daylight hours lengthen.
- Fertilize monthly with a diluted, balanced fertilizer.
- Allow for more light, but still avoid full sun.
- Encourage fuller growth by rotating the plant for even light exposure.

Fall: Bloom Preparation

- Reduce watering slightly and stop fertilizing in late September.
- Provide cooler night temperatures (50–55°F if possible).
- Begin controlling light exposure to mimic short days.
- Avoid moving or disturbing the plant once buds form—this can cause them to drop.

Winter: Bloom and Recovery

- Water sparingly but don't allow the soil to dry out completely.
- Avoid repotting or pruning during bloom.

- Remove spent flowers gently to encourage new bud formation.
- Once flowering ends, allow the plant to enter a light rest period.

Adjusting Watering with the Season

- In summer: Water thoroughly when the top inch of soil is dry.
- In winter: Allow the top third of the pot to dry before watering again.
- Avoid overwatering in cooler months—this is the most common cause of root and stem rot.

Lighting Through the Year

- In winter, move the plant closer to a window to compensate for reduced natural light.
- In summer, pull it back or add sheer curtains to avoid sunburn.

By responding to seasonal cues, your plant will remain in sync with its natural growth and flowering rhythm— ultimately leading to better performance and fewer care issues.

Dormancy Period Requirements

Though not a full dormancy in the way some perennials behave, Christmas Cactus undergoes a **quasi-dormant phase** that is essential to healthy blooming. This "rest" period mimics the natural environmental pause before flowering.

41

What Is Dormancy in Christmas Cactus?

Dormancy is a period of **slowed metabolic activity**, during which the plant conserves energy, reduces growth, and prepares for flower development. This typically occurs in **late fall to early winter**, following a period of gradual darkness and cooler temperatures.

Triggers for Dormancy and Bud Formation

- **Reduced daylight**: Shorter days naturally cue the plant to rest.
- **Lower temperatures**: Ideal range is 50–55°F (10–13°C) at night.
- **Dryer soil**: Water less frequently to signal rest mode.
- **No feeding**: Fertilizer during this time can hinder the dormancy process.

How Long Should Dormancy Last?

- Aim for **4 to 6 weeks** of reduced light and cooler temperatures.
- This period usually begins in late October or early November.
- During this time, do not prune, repot, or propagate.

What Happens If You Skip Dormancy?

- The plant may continue to grow but **fail to bloom**.
- Blooming may occur sporadically or not at all.
- Buds may form but then **drop prematurely** if the transition was incomplete or disrupted.

Post-Dormancy Bloom Cycle

Once buds begin to form:

- Return the plant to warmer temperatures (65°F to 70°F).
- Resume normal watering as needed to support bud development.
- Continue bright, indirect light exposure.
- Do not move the plant unnecessarily—bud drop is often triggered by relocation stress.

The dormancy period may seem counterintuitive—after all, it involves doing *less*—but it is one of the most important phases in Christmas Cactus care. Those who learn to respect this cycle are consistently rewarded with beautiful, reliable blooms.

Providing the ideal indoor growing conditions for a Christmas Cactus is more about balance than precision. It's about emulating the gentle rhythms of its tropical forest origins—cool but not cold, humid but not soggy, bright but not blinding, and restful at just the right time.

By mastering the interplay between temperature, humidity, light, air movement, and seasonal change, any grower can unlock the full potential of this remarkable plant. The result is a healthier cactus, more vibrant blooms, and the satisfaction of seeing your plant not just survive, but **flourish in your home year after year.**

CHAPTER TWO

POTTING AND SOIL ESSENTIALS

The long-term health of your Christmas Cactus depends significantly on what lies beneath the surface: its pot and soil environment. While these plants are low-maintenance in many ways, improper potting or poor soil choices can lead to root rot, poor growth, and ultimately plant decline. Because the Christmas Cactus is a **tropical epiphyte** with delicate roots adapted for moisture-rich but well-aerated environments, creating the correct potting conditions is essential. **Choosing the Right Pot Size and Type**

The container you select for your Christmas Cactus has a direct impact on root health, watering frequency, stability, and long-term vitality. While this plant is adaptable and can grow in a variety of vessels, some general guidelines help ensure success.

1. Sizing Guidelines
Christmas Cactus prefers to be **slightly root-bound** and typically performs better in a snug pot than in one that is overly large. A pot that's too big retains excess moisture, increasing the risk of **root rot** and fungal infections.

- When potting a young plant or propagated cutting: use a **4 to 6-inch pot.**

- For mature plants or those being repotted: choose a pot **only 1 to 2 inches wider** than the current root ball.
- Shallow pots are preferred over deep pots since the plant's roots are relatively shallow.

2. Material Considerations
Pots come in various materials, and each affects moisture retention and air movement differently.

- **Terracotta (unglazed clay)**: Porous and allows for airflow and evaporation. Ideal for beginners who tend to overwater. However, it dries out faster, especially in low-humidity environments.
- **Plastic pots**: Hold moisture longer, which can be beneficial in dry climates. Lightweight and inexpensive but require careful monitoring to prevent soggy soil.
- **Ceramic pots (with drainage holes)**: Combine aesthetic appeal with functionality. Glazed ceramics slow water loss but should still include proper drainage.
- **Self-watering pots**: Not ideal unless modified, as they can keep the soil too wet for Christmas Cactus.

3. Drainage is Non-Negotiable
Every container, regardless of size or material, must have **adequate drainage holes**. Waterlogged roots are the fastest route to decay and fungal infection in Christmas Cactus. If using decorative cachepots without holes, ensure the growing pot inside can drain freely and be removed for watering.

4. Visual and Practical Design
Hanging pots and elevated stands work well due to the plant's **trailing growth habit**, especially when in

45

bloom. Choose wide-based pots to prevent tipping, especially as the plant matures and becomes top-heavy with flowers.

The Ideal Soil Mix: Drainage and Aeration

Choosing or creating the right soil is as important as the container itself. In its native habitat, the Christmas Cactus grows on tree branches in a mixture of **moss, decomposing leaves, and organic debris**—not dense soil. This epiphytic nature means that its roots demand excellent drainage and airflow.

1. Traits of a Good Christmas Cactus Mix

- **Well-draining**: Prevents water from pooling around the roots
- **Lightweight**: Supports the delicate, fibrous root structure
- **Aerated**: Contains ingredients that maintain space for oxygen flow
- **Slightly acidic**: A pH of **5.5 to 6.2** is ideal

2. Components of an Ideal Mix
  A good potting medium can be store-bought (cactus or succulent mix) or homemade using common ingredients. The ideal mix should not compact over time and must strike the right balance between moisture retention and aeration.

Basic DIY Christmas Cactus Soil Mix

- **2 parts potting soil** (peat- or coco coir-based)
- **1 part perlite or pumice** (to increase drainage)

- **1 part orchid bark or coconut husk chips** (adds structure and mimics epiphytic conditions)

Optional Add-ins

- **Compost** (small amounts): Adds nutrients and supports healthy microbiota.
- **Horticultural sand**: Further improves drainage but should not exceed 20% of the mix.
- **Worm castings**: For light organic enrichment.

Avoid These Soil Types

- **Garden soil**: Too heavy, compacts easily, and may introduce pests.
- **Plain peat moss**: Can become hydrophobic (repels water) when dry.
- **Soil mixes with water-retaining crystals**: These increase the risk of root rot.

Prepackaged Potting Mix Tips

If using commercial cactus or succulent mixes, consider amending them with extra perlite and bark to increase porosity. Many store-bought versions are designed for desert cacti and may hold too much moisture for tropical species like *Schlumbergera*.

Re-potting Guidelines and Timing

Christmas Cactus is a slow-growing plant that does not need frequent repotting. In fact, these plants often bloom more prolifically when slightly root-bound. However, repotting becomes necessary when roots fill the container, the soil becomes compacted, or the plant shows signs of stress.

When to Repot

- **Every 3 to 4 years**, or when the root ball visibly outgrows the container
- **After flowering ends** in late winter or early spring (ideal time for minimal stress)
- If water drains poorly or the soil appears moldy or overly compacted
- If the plant shows signs of being root-bound (explained further below)

Steps to Repot a Christmas Cactus

1. **Prepare the new pot**: Ensure it's clean, has drainage, and is only slightly larger.
2. **Remove the plant gently**: Support the base and ease the plant out of its current pot. Avoid tugging or forcing.
3. **Inspect the roots**: Trim any black, mushy, or dead roots with sterilized scissors.
4. **Shake off old soil**: Especially if it's compacted or moldy. Retain some of the healthy mix around roots.
5. **Position and fill**: Place the plant at the same depth as before and backfill with fresh mix.
6. **Water lightly**: Allow the soil to settle but do not soak. Wait 5–7 days before resuming normal watering.

Aftercare

- Place the newly repotted plant in indirect light.

- Avoid fertilizing for 4–6 weeks to allow root recovery.
- Watch for transplant shock (wilting, slow growth), which is temporary if care conditions are good.

Signs of Root Bound Plants

Being slightly root-bound is not harmful and is even favorable for blooming. However, a severely root-bound plant can experience stunted growth, dehydration, and structural instability. Recognizing the signs early helps you repot before damage sets in.

Visual and Physical Symptoms

- **Roots circling the pot**: When you remove the plant, you'll see dense root spirals around the perimeter.
- **Water drains too quickly**: Water rushes through the soil but leaves the plant dry, as roots occupy all available space.
- **Wilting despite regular watering**: Indicates poor moisture retention due to excessive root crowding.
- **Bulging or cracked pots**: In clay pots, roots may push so hard they deform the container.
- **Growth slows or stops**: Once the roots are out of space, above-ground growth halts.
- **Increased leaf drop or bud drop**: Stress from root confinement can lead to premature shedding.

Gently loosening the root ball before repotting helps encourage the roots to spread into fresh soil. Severely matted roots may need light pruning to stimulate healthy regrowth.

Common Potting Mistakes to Avoid

Even with the best intentions, many plant owners encounter issues by making preventable potting errors. Here are the most frequent mistakes and how to avoid them:

1. Using Oversized Pots

- **Problem**: Too much space retains moisture and delays drying time.
- **Solution**: Only upsize by 1 to 2 inches in diameter when repotting.

2. Poor Drainage

- **Problem**: Water accumulates at the base, suffocating roots.
- **Solution**: Always use pots with holes and a well-draining soil mix. Never rely on rocks at the bottom as a substitute for drainage.

3. Frequent Repotting

- **Problem**: Disturbs roots unnecessarily and can lead to stress.
- **Solution**: Only repot every few years or when signs of root binding appear.

4. Heavy, Compacted Soil

- **Problem**: Limits oxygen, leading to root rot and fungus.

- **Solution**: Amend soil with perlite, bark, or sand to increase airflow.

5. Ignoring Root Health During Repotting

- **Problem**: Leaving behind rotten roots or failing to inspect for pests.
- **Solution**: Always clean and examine roots thoroughly during repotting.

6. Potting During Bloom

- **Problem**: Causes bud drop or bloom failure.
- **Solution**: Repot only after the flowering cycle is complete, typically in late winter or early spring.

7. Top-Heavy Containers

- **Problem**: Can tip over and damage the plant.
- **Solution**: Use wide-based pots for stability or secure the container with a weight in hanging baskets.

8. Forgetting to Let Soil Rest After Repotting

- **Problem**: Watering immediately can cause rot in freshly disturbed roots.
- **Solution**: Wait about a week before resuming regular watering to let roots heal.

By avoiding these pitfalls, plant owners can create a supportive root environment that encourages healthy growth, consistent flowering, and resilience against pests and disease.

Potting and soil care are foundational to the success of your Christmas Cactus. When you understand how this unique plant has evolved—clinging to tree branches in a damp yet airy rainforest environment—you can better replicate those conditions at home.

By choosing the right pot size and material, building a light and breathable soil mix, knowing when and how to repot, and avoiding common mistakes, you empower your Christmas Cactus to thrive for years—if not decades. A well-potted plant is easier to care for, blooms more reliably, and resists the stressors that lead to decline.

WATERING THE RIGHT WAY

For many plant owners, watering seems like the simplest part of plant care. Yet, when it comes to the Christmas Cactus (*Schlumbergera* × *buckleyi*), watering is both an art and a science. Unlike desert cacti, this tropical epiphyte hails from the misty, shaded forests of Brazil, where moisture is abundant but never stagnant. In its native environment, rainwater drips steadily through the forest canopy, moistening the leaf litter and moss in which the cactus anchors itself.

Replicating these nuanced moisture conditions indoors is vital to the health, growth, and flowering cycle of your Christmas Cactus. In this chapter, we will examine how often to water, how to adjust watering routines by season, how water quality affects plant health, how to recognize overwatering and underwatering, and how to prevent root rot—a leading cause of plant death in *Schlumbergera*.

How Often Should You Water?

There is no universal watering schedule that applies to all Christmas Cactus plants, because watering needs depend on several environmental variables:

- **Temperature** (higher temps = faster evaporation)
- **Humidity levels** (dry air increases water loss)
- **Light exposure** (more light = higher water usage)
- **Pot size and material** (smaller pots and clay pots dry out faster)
- **Soil composition** (fast-draining mixes require more frequent watering)

Despite these variables, a few general principles apply.

General Watering Frequency

- **During active growth (spring and summer)**: Every 5 to 10 days. Water when the top 1 to 2 inches of soil feels dry to the touch.
- **During fall bloom preparation**: Water less frequently—every 10 to 14 days—to simulate seasonal drought and stimulate bud formation.
- **During winter bloom**: Resume moderate watering (every 7 to 10 days), but never let the soil become soggy.
- **After flowering (dormancy phase)**: Water sparingly—approximately every 2 to 3 weeks, or when soil is dry one-third down.

The Finger Test Method

Use your index finger to test the soil. Insert it about one inch into the soil:

- If the soil feels dry, it's time to water.
- If it feels cool or moist, wait a few days.

A moisture meter can also provide more accurate readings, especially for beginners unsure about judging soil dryness by touch.

Important Rule of Thumb

It's **better to slightly underwater** a Christmas Cactus than to overwater it. These plants can recover from minor droughts more easily than from root rot caused by excessive moisture.

Seasonal Watering Adjustments

Just as the plant's growth and flowering cycles shift with the seasons, so too must your watering habits. Many Christmas Cactus owners make the mistake of watering on a fixed schedule year-round, which can cause stress during sensitive stages such as dormancy or bud formation.

Spring and Early Summer (Growth Phase)

- Increase watering as light and warmth increase.
- Water thoroughly once the top inch of soil is dry.
- Fertilization resumes, and moisture is needed to support nutrient uptake.

54

- Avoid allowing the plant to dry out completely for extended periods.

Late Summer to Fall (Pre-Bloom Phase)

- Begin reducing water in late August or September.
- Mimic the natural dry season of its native environment.
- The reduction in water, combined with longer nights and cooler temperatures, signals the plant to prepare for blooming.

Fall and Early Winter (Bloom Phase)

- Resume moderate watering when buds form.
- Keep the soil lightly moist—not saturated—to support bud development.
- Avoid letting the plant dry out completely, as this can cause buds to drop prematurely.
- Do not mist heavily during bloom, as flowers are sensitive to moisture and may decay.

Post-Bloom Rest Period (Late Winter)

- Once flowering ends, reduce watering again.
- Provide only enough moisture to keep the plant from shriveling.
- Overwatering during this stage may delay or prevent the plant from re-entering the growth cycle in spring.

Adjusting your watering with the natural rhythm of the seasons helps synchronize the plant's internal cycle with its external environment, resulting in a healthier, more predictable bloom cycle.

Water Quality: What to Use or Avoid

While many people focus on **when** to water their Christmas Cactus, **what kind of water** you use is just as important. The sensitive root systems of tropical cacti can react negatively to certain water additives or mineral levels, particularly when watering over a long period of time.

Best Water Options

1. **Rainwater**

- Closest to what the plant would receive in the wild.
- Naturally soft, slightly acidic, and free from treatment chemicals.

2. **Distilled Water**

- Completely purified and safe from salts, chlorine, and heavy metals.
- Ideal for long-term watering in areas with hard tap water.

3. **Filtered Water (Carbon or Reverse Osmosis)**

- Removes chlorine, chloramines, fluoride, and many minerals.
- Good compromise between convenience and plant safety.

56

Water Temperature Tips

- Always use **room temperature water** to avoid shocking the roots.
- Cold water can cause contraction of plant cells, while warm water can encourage fungal growth.

Water to Avoid

1. **Hard Tap Water**

- Contains calcium, magnesium, and salt deposits that build up in the soil over time.
- Can raise soil pH and inhibit nutrient uptake.

2. **Softened Water**

- Treated with sodium, which is harmful to plant roots.
- Leads to salt accumulation and root burn.

3. **Water with Fertilizer Residue**

- Leftover water containing undiluted fertilizer can damage roots.
- Always mix fertilizers fresh and avoid using residual feed water.

If you must use tap water, allow it to **sit overnight in an open container** to help dissipate chlorine. However, this does not remove fluoride or chloramine, which require filtration.

Regular flushing of the soil with distilled water can also help leach out accumulated minerals and prevent long-term damage.

Signs of Overwatering vs. Underwatering

Learning to recognize the signs of improper watering is a crucial skill in Christmas Cactus care. Since symptoms of both overwatering and underwatering can look similar at a glance, it's essential to understand the subtle differences.

Signs of Overwatering

- **Yellowing stem segments**, particularly at the base.
- **Soft, mushy texture** in the lower stem or near the soil line.
- **Foul odor** from the soil, indicating root rot.
- **Buds dropping** without opening, especially in fall or winter.
- Soil feels **wet for days**, and drainage is poor.

Overwatered plants often develop **blackened or translucent segments**, a sign of rot setting in. If not corrected, the rot may travel upward, eventually killing the plant.

Signs of Underwatering

- **Wrinkled or shriveled segments**, especially on the ends.
- Plant appears **limp or wilted**, even though stems are dry.
- Growth is **slow**, and new segments are stunted.
- **Segment edges curl inward**, indicating dehydration.
- Soil feels completely **dry and pulls away from the pot edges**.

Unlike overwatering, underwatering damage is more easily reversed. Simply resuming a normal watering routine can restore turgor pressure (firmness) in the stems within a few days.

Troubleshooting Tip

If you're unsure whether the plant is overwatered or underwatered, remove the plant gently from its pot and inspect the roots:

- **Healthy roots**: White or light tan and firm.
- **Rotting roots**: Black, brown, or mushy with a foul smell.
- **Dry roots**: Brittle and wiry, often with compacted dry soil clinging to them.

Adjust watering based on your findings. In cases of root rot, pruning affected areas and repotting in fresh soil is often necessary.

Best Practices for Preventing Root Rot

Root rot is the leading cause of death in Christmas Cactus. It can set in quickly and often goes unnoticed until the plant shows advanced symptoms. The good news is that it's completely preventable with the right approach to watering and soil management.

1. Always Use Well-Draining Soil
Avoid soils that retain too much moisture. Use a blend with perlite, orchid bark, or pumice to ensure that water moves quickly through the pot and doesn't stagnate around the roots.

2. Choose the Right Pot
Ensure the pot has **sufficient drainage holes**. Avoid decorative pots without holes unless used only as outer covers (with the actual plant in a grow pot that can be removed for watering).

3. Let Soil Dry Between Waterings
Do not water on a calendar schedule. Check the soil moisture manually, and only water when the top inch is dry. Remember that this timing will shift with the seasons.

4. Avoid Watering at Night
Water early in the day so that excess moisture has time to evaporate. Nighttime watering in cool conditions increases the risk of fungal growth.

5. Empty Drainage Trays Immediately
Do not allow pots to sit in standing water. After watering, wait 15–30 minutes and then empty any water collected in trays or outer containers.

6. Be Cautious After Repotting
Newly repotted plants need time to heal. Wait 5 to 7

days after repotting before resuming watering, and then water lightly at first.

7. Use Fungicide if Necessary

If the plant has been overwatered but is not yet rotting, a **preventive antifungal drench** can help protect roots. Use only if recommended and with proper dilution.

8. Monitor Humidity and Airflow

Excessive humidity with poor air movement encourages fungal growth. Use a small fan in enclosed spaces or increase ventilation during humid seasons.

9. Avoid Misting the Soil Surface

While misting can increase humidity, do not mist the soil itself, as it can lead to the growth of algae and fungus. Focus on increasing ambient humidity through trays or room humidifiers.

Watering may seem like a basic task, but for Christmas Cactus, it is a core element of its health and bloom performance. By learning **how often to water**, understanding **how seasonal needs shift**, using **clean, safe water**, spotting the early signs of moisture imbalance, and **preventing root rot**, you lay the groundwork for long-lasting success with this unique and rewarding plant.

Watering the right way means tuning into your plant's environment and rhythm—responding to it rather than imposing a rigid schedule. With just a little observation and adjustment, your Christmas Cactus will reward you with lush green segments and brilliant seasonal blooms that brighten the darkest days of winter.

CHAPTER THREE

FEEDING FOR STRONG GROWTH AND BLOOMS

Feeding your Christmas Cactus properly is a crucial but often overlooked part of its long-term care. While these plants are known for their hardiness and ability to survive in less-than-ideal conditions, thriving and **reliably blooming year after year** requires attention to their nutritional needs. A well-fed Christmas Cactus will display vigorous growth, firm and vibrant segments, and a profusion of healthy flowers each season. **Nutritional Needs of Christmas Cactus**

The Christmas Cactus, while not heavy feeders, still depends on a consistent supply of essential nutrients to sustain healthy growth, tissue repair, root development, and flowering. These nutrients, both macro and micronutrients, play distinct roles in the plant's physiological processes.

1. Macronutrients
The three primary nutrients required by all plants are nitrogen (N), phosphorus (P), and potassium (K), commonly represented as the N-P-K ratio on fertilizer labels.

- **Nitrogen (N)**: Encourages leafy, green growth and supports photosynthesis. For Christmas Cactus, nitrogen helps produce healthy stem segments (cladodes), which are the primary photosynthetic organs.

- **Phosphorus (P)**: Promotes strong root development and supports flowering and fruiting. Phosphorus is crucial for bud formation and overall reproductive health.
- **Potassium (K)**: Supports overall plant health, disease resistance, and flower durability. It regulates water uptake and strengthens tissue.

2. Secondary Macronutrients

- **Calcium (Ca)**: Aids in cell wall development and root structure.
- **Magnesium (Mg)**: Central to chlorophyll production and energy transfer.
- **Sulfur (S)**: Needed for protein synthesis and enzyme function.

3. Micronutrients
Though needed in smaller quantities, micronutrients such as **iron, manganese, boron, zinc, copper, and molybdenum** are vital for enzymatic reactions, hormone function, and pigment development.

Without proper feeding, the Christmas Cactus may show symptoms such as:

- **Pale or yellowing segments** (nitrogen or magnesium deficiency)
- **Stunted growth or small segments** (phosphorus or calcium deficiency)

- **Poor bud formation or flower drop** (lack of potassium or trace nutrients)

Best Fertilizer Formulas and Schedules

Once you understand what nutrients your plant needs, the next step is choosing a fertilizer that delivers those nutrients in the proper balance. Fertilizers are available in liquid, granular, and slow-release forms. For indoor potted plants like the Christmas Cactus, **liquid or water-soluble fertilizers** are the most easily absorbed and controlled.

1. Ideal Fertilizer Ratio
A balanced fertilizer such as **10-10-10** or **20-20-20** is appropriate for general use. However, many growers prefer a **bloom-supporting formula** once buds begin forming. These include:

- **Low-nitrogen, high-phosphorus options**: e.g., 5-10-10 or 2-7-7
- These help shift the plant's energy from vegetative growth to bud production and flower development.

2. Feeding Schedule by Season

- **Early Spring to Mid-Summer (Growth Phase)**
  o Use a balanced fertilizer (e.g., 10-10-10) every **4 weeks**.
  o Dilute to **half strength** to avoid overfeeding sensitive roots.
  o This is when the plant produces new segments and expands its root system.
- **Late Summer to Early Fall (Pre-Bloom Phase)**

- o Switch to a bloom-boosting formula (e.g., 5-10-10).
- o Feed every **4 weeks** until flower buds appear.
- o Reduce nitrogen to prevent leggy growth and promote bud formation.
- **Fall Blooming Period**
- o Fertilize **once** at the beginning of bloom formation, then stop.
- o Excess nutrients during blooming can cause **bud drop** or distort flower shape.
- **Winter Rest Period (Post-Bloom)**
- o Suspend all feeding during dormancy (typically 4–6 weeks).
- o Resume in late winter or early spring with diluted balanced fertilizer.

3. Dilution and Application Tips

- Always **water the plant before fertilizing** to avoid root burn.
- Use **diluted fertilizer**—half the recommended strength unless otherwise directed.
- Apply directly to the soil, avoiding contact with the plant stems or segments.

Fertilizing in small, regular doses is more effective than infrequent, heavy feedings, which can stress the plant and lead to salt buildup in the soil.

How to Feed During Blooming Season

Feeding during the blooming season requires a shift in strategy. At this stage, the plant is investing energy in producing flowers, and the wrong type or timing of fertilizer can interrupt or weaken the bloom.

1. Pre-Bloom (Late Summer to Early Fall)

- Use a **low-nitrogen, higher phosphorus and potassium formula** to support bud initiation.
- Feed once at the beginning of September, then again in early October if buds haven't yet appeared.
- Stop feeding once flower buds are visible.

2. Active Blooming (Late Fall to Early Winter)

- **Do not fertilize regularly during bloom**. The plant is in a delicate physiological state, and additional nutrients can disturb the balance.
- If you must feed, use a very diluted solution (quarter strength) and only once during early bloom.
- Avoid any fertilizer with high nitrogen content during this phase.

3. Flower Maintenance Tips

- Provide steady moisture (not wet soil) to support flower longevity.
- Avoid drafts or sudden temperature changes, which can interfere with nutrient uptake and trigger bud drop.

4. Post-Bloom Recovery (Late Winter)

- Wait until flowers are fully spent and removed before resuming feeding.
- Use a balanced fertilizer to support root recovery and prepare for the next growth phase.

Fertilizing during the bloom phase is all about **supporting the plant without overstimulating it**. It's a time to reduce nutrient load and let the plant focus its energy on flowering.

Organic Feeding Options

Organic feeding is ideal for gardeners who prefer natural methods, want to avoid synthetic chemical buildup, or are growing in eco-conscious environments. Organic fertilizers release nutrients slowly, improve soil structure, and support microbial health.

1. Organic Liquid Fertilizers

- **Fish emulsion**: Rich in nitrogen, useful in early spring.
- **Seaweed extract**: Provides potassium and trace elements, promotes root strength and flowering.
- **Compost tea**: Balanced nutrition, improves microbial activity and root health.

2. Solid Organic Options

- **Worm castings**: Gentle and rich in trace nutrients; mix into soil or top-dress.
- **Bone meal**: High in phosphorus; supports bloom production.

- **Kelp meal**: Slow-release potassium and micronutrients.
- **Bat guano (low-nitrogen blend)**: Excellent pre-bloom booster; apply sparingly.

3. How to Use Organics with Christmas Cactus

- Mix dry ingredients into the top layer of soil before watering.
- Dilute liquid organics to half or quarter strength to avoid overfeeding.
- Combine with **monthly flushing of soil** to prevent salt buildup, even if natural.

4. Benefits of Organic Feeding

- Less risk of nutrient burn or overdose
- Long-term improvement of soil quality
- Encouragement of beneficial fungi and bacteria
- More sustainable and safer around pets and children

While organic fertilizers may act more slowly than synthetic options, they offer a more **balanced, long-term approach** to plant health and bloom resilience.

Feeding Mistakes That Hinder Blooming

Even with good intentions, many growers make feeding mistakes that inadvertently prevent their Christmas Cactus from blooming—or worse, contribute to disease and decline. Below are the most common errors and how to correct or avoid them.

1. Over-Fertilizing

- Problem: Excess salts accumulate in the soil, damaging roots and preventing bud development.
- Symptoms: Brown tips, wilting despite watering, poor flower production.
- Solution: Always dilute fertilizer. Flush the soil monthly with clean water to remove residue.

2. Feeding at the Wrong Time

- Problem: Fertilizing during dormancy or peak bloom can confuse the plant's cycle.
- Symptoms: Buds drop, growth appears weak or unseasonal.
- Solution: Follow the plant's rhythm—feed during active growth and reduce or pause during bloom.

3. Using High-Nitrogen Fertilizer Year-Round

- Problem: Too much nitrogen promotes leafy growth at the expense of flowering.
- Symptoms: Lush green segments but no blooms.
- Solution: Switch to a bloom formula with low nitrogen in late summer.

4. Applying Fertilizer to Dry Soil

- Problem: Nutrient concentration increases around dry roots, causing chemical burns.
- Symptoms: Scorched roots, stunted growth, leaf drop.
- Solution: Always water the plant before applying fertilizer.

5. Ignoring Soil Type

- Problem: Fertilizer behaves differently in compacted or poor-draining soils.
- Symptoms: Fertilizer runoff, root damage, inconsistent nutrient uptake.
- Solution: Use a light, well-draining soil mix to allow even fertilizer distribution.

6. Using Expired or Improperly Stored Fertilizers

- Problem: Old fertilizer may lose potency or become imbalanced.
- Solution: Store in a cool, dry place and check expiration dates before use.

7. Failing to Adjust with Environmental Changes

- Problem: Fertilizer needs change with temperature, light, and humidity.
- Solution: Adjust your feeding schedule and formulation with the seasons, just as you would your watering habits.

Avoiding these common pitfalls ensures that your feeding regimen enhances, rather than disrupts, the plant's natural cycle.

Feeding a Christmas Cactus correctly involves far more than simply adding fertilizer to the pot every few weeks. It requires **timing, balance, and observation**. By understanding the plant's nutritional needs throughout the year, using the right fertilizer formulations, adjusting feeding strategies based on seasonal cycles, and avoiding common mistakes, you give your plant the tools to flourish.

Healthy feeding practices produce **robust root systems, vibrant green segments, and profuse blooms** that make the Christmas Cactus a centerpiece of your indoor garden. Whether you prefer synthetic or organic options, the key is to work with the plant's natural rhythms—not against them.

ENCOURAGING SPECTACULAR HOLIDAY BLOOMS

One of the most enchanting qualities of the Christmas Cactus (*Schlumbergera* × *buckleyi*) is its ability to produce stunning, pendulous blooms right when the rest of nature is asleep—during the coldest, darkest months of the year. Its flowers can brighten the heart of winter and turn any windowsill into a festive, living display. But for many plant owners, encouraging these holiday blooms consistently remains a mystery.

Unlike many houseplants, the Christmas Cactus requires a **combination of environmental triggers**—specifically related to light, temperature, and seasonal shifts—to initiate and sustain flowering. In this chapter, we will explore the *natural bloom cycle*, how to use **light and darkness** to your advantage, the importance of **temperature fluctuations**, strategies to ensure **re-blooming year after year**, and solutions to troubleshoot **non-blooming plants.**

Understanding the Natural Bloom Cycle

To understand how to encourage blooming, we must first understand how and why it happens in the plant's life cycle. Christmas Cactus is a **photoperiodic plant**, meaning its bloom cycle is triggered by **day length and environmental cues** rather than just age or size.

1. Native Climate and Natural Cues

In its native Brazilian habitat, the Christmas Cactus experiences:

- **Cooler nights** in the fall
- **Shorter daylight hours**
- **Decreased rainfall before blooming**
- **Gradual transition into a drier, cooler season**

These environmental changes signal to the plant that it's time to prepare for reproduction. In the wild, flowering at this time ensures pollinators are active and conditions are right for seed development. As a result, the plant has evolved to bloom not randomly, but **in response to very specific conditions**.

2. The Three Main Phases of the Bloom Cycle

1. **Preparation (Late Summer to Early Fall):** Growth slows down. The plant begins conserving energy for bud formation. Watering and feeding should be reduced during this stage to replicate the natural "dry season."
2. **Bud Initiation (Fall):** Triggered by short days, cool nights, and a drop in moisture. This is the most critical stage in the cycle. Interruption in these conditions often leads to bud failure.

73

3. **Blooming (Winter Holidays):** After successful bud formation, the plant enters full bloom, which can last from **2 to 6 weeks**, depending on care and variety.

Understanding this cycle empowers growers to **mimic it indoors** and encourage reliable holiday blooming.

Light and Darkness Triggers for Flowering

Perhaps the most misunderstood and misapplied factor in Christmas Cactus blooming is the role of **photoperiodism,** or how the plant responds to light and darkness.

1. Short-Day Plant Behavior

Christmas Cactus is a **short-day plant,** which means it requires **long periods of uninterrupted darkness** (typically 12–14 hours per night) for several consecutive weeks to initiate flowering. This distinguishes it from long-day or day-neutral plants that bloom based on other cues.

- **Day length** must be **12 hours or less** for at least **4 to 6 consecutive weeks**.
- Darkness must be **uninterrupted**—even brief exposure to artificial light at night can reset the plant's internal clock.

2. How to Control Light Indoors

For most indoor growers, the best way to manage light and darkness is through a combination of **location control** and **manual coverage**.

Option A: Natural Light Regulation

- Place the plant in a **room with natural light only** (e.g., a guest room or office that isn't used in the evenings).
- Avoid turning on overhead lights at night.

Option B: Manual Light Blocking

- If your home is well-lit at night, cover the plant with a **box or opaque bag** from early evening to morning.
- Ensure complete darkness during the "night" period— no TV, lamps, or hallway lights.

3. Light Requirements After Bud Formation

Once flower buds have formed:

- **Stop light manipulation.**
- Return the plant to a brighter location with **indirect sunlight** to encourage bloom development.
- Keep the light steady, as moving the plant frequently during this stage can cause **bud drop**.

4. Warning Signs of Improper Lighting

- No blooms despite healthy growth: too much nighttime light.
- Buds form then fall off: inconsistent lighting or drafts.
- Excessive leafy growth and no flowers: too much nitrogen or inadequate darkness.

75

By aligning the plant's light exposure with its natural rhythm, you can trigger the internal flowering response with great success—even in a controlled indoor environment.

Temperature's Role in Bud Development

Temperature is just as critical as light in prompting the Christmas Cactus to bloom. It works in conjunction with short-day triggers, helping the plant interpret seasonal change.

1. Ideal Temperatures for Bud Initiation

The Christmas Cactus prefers:

- **Day temperatures** between **60°F and 70°F (15°C to 21°C)**
- **Night temperatures** between **50°F and 55°F (10°C to 13°C)**

These cooler night temperatures simulate the onset of fall in its native environment and **signal the plant to begin reproductive growth.**

2. Cold Stress vs. Chill Trigger

It's important to distinguish between **controlled cool temperatures** and **cold stress:**

- Controlled cool temps aid flowering.
- Exposure to **frost or freezing** will **damage buds or kill the plant.**

3. Best Practices for Temperature Control

- Place the plant near a **cool, draft-free window** (east- or north-facing).
- In climates where outdoor night temps drop to 50–55°F, consider **placing the plant outdoors** for 2–3 weeks in early fall to naturally trigger blooming.
- Avoid sudden temperature changes (e.g., placing near a heater after a cool period).

4. After Bud Formation

Once buds appear, move the plant to a **slightly warmer area** (around 65–70°F) to support healthy flower development. Do not expose it to temperatures above 75°F or below 50°F during this stage.

5. Warning Signs of Temperature Imbalance

- Buds form but fall prematurely: too warm or too dry.
- Delayed bloom: insufficient cool nights.
- No buds despite darkness: night temperatures are staying too high.

The correct **temperature drop**, paired with reduced light, is what most reliably initiates the blooming cycle.

Encouraging Re-blooming Year After Year

A healthy Christmas Cactus can live for decades and rebloom annually when cared for correctly. Re-blooming is a combination of **good year-round maintenance** and timely environmental manipulation in late summer to fall.

1. Post-Bloom Recovery (January–March)

- Remove spent flowers gently by hand.
- Prune leggy growth to promote fuller shape and future flowering.
- Allow the plant a brief **rest period**—water sparingly, stop feeding, and place in indirect light.

2. Active Growth Phase (Spring–Summer)

- Resume feeding with a **balanced fertilizer** every 4–6 weeks.
- Provide bright but indirect light.
- Maintain room temperatures between 65°F and 75°F.
- Water when the top inch of soil dries out.

3. Pre-Bloom Preparation (August–September)

- Reduce watering to simulate a "dry season."
- Stop fertilizing in early September.
- Introduce 12–14 hours of darkness and cooler nights.
- Maintain this for **4 to 6 weeks** to trigger bud formation.

4. Bud Development and Bloom (October–December)

- Move the plant to brighter indirect light once buds form.
- Increase watering slightly to support bud development.
- Do not repot, prune, or relocate the plant during this time.
- Rotate the plant gently every few days to encourage symmetrical blooming.

5. Long-Term Tips for Annual Blooming

- Use the same lighting and temperature manipulation **every fall**.
- Avoid skipping the cool period—even one year of improper conditions can disrupt future blooming.
- Keep records of what worked well—bloom time, lighting schedules, feeding habits—to replicate the process.

What to Do if Your Cactus Won't Bloom

Even with good intentions, sometimes a Christmas Cactus simply won't flower. This can be frustrating, especially when the plant appears healthy otherwise. Fortunately, bloom failure is usually caused by **a few identifiable factors**, most of which can be corrected.

1. Inadequate Darkness

- **Problem**: The plant is exposed to artificial light at night (TVs, lamps, hallway lights).
- **Solution**: Provide complete darkness for 12–14 hours daily for 4–6 weeks.

2. Warm Night Temperatures

- **Problem**: The plant never experiences the cool nights needed to trigger budding.
- **Solution**: Expose the plant to cooler conditions— ideally 50–55°F at night.

3. Overfertilization with Nitrogen

- **Problem**: High-nitrogen fertilizer promotes leaf growth instead of blooming.
- **Solution**: Use low-nitrogen, high-phosphorus bloom formulas in late summer.

4. Inconsistent Environment

- **Problem**: Frequent moving, drafts, or erratic watering during bud formation.
- **Solution**: Create a stable environment during the critical pre-bloom and bloom phases.

5. Age or Size of the Plant

- **Problem**: Very young or recently propagated cuttings may not yet be ready to bloom.
- **Solution**: Allow a full year of growth before expecting reliable flowering.

6. Overwatering or Poor Drainage

- **Problem**: Roots are suffocating or rotting, weakening the plant.
- **Solution**: Adjust watering habits and consider repotting into a well-draining soil mix.

7. Lack of Dormancy Period

- **Problem**: The plant never had a "rest" period between bloom cycles.

- **Solution**: Allow 4–6 weeks of cooler, drier conditions after flowering ends.

Troubleshooting Strategy

If your plant refuses to bloom:

- Reset its environmental clock by giving it **6 full weeks of dark nights and cool temperatures**.
- Pause feeding and reduce watering.
- Once buds appear, return to moderate light and resume watering.

In most cases, **bloom failure is reversible** with patience and consistent care.

Encouraging spectacular holiday blooms from your Christmas Cactus is not a matter of chance—it's a carefully orchestrated dance between **light, temperature, moisture, and timing**. By understanding its natural bloom cycle, providing long nights and cool temperatures at the right time, and managing your plant's environment with intention, you can reliably trigger flowering each year.

With these techniques in hand, your Christmas Cactus can become a cherished seasonal tradition—blooming year after year as a living symbol of patience, beauty, and renewal.

PRUNING AND SHAPING TECHNIQUES

Pruning a Christmas Cactus (*Schlumbergera* × *buckleyi*) is often seen as optional, but in truth, it's a **vital part of maintaining plant health, shape, and bloom quality** over time. While these tropical cacti don't require constant intervention, strategic pruning can transform a leggy, tired plant into a vibrant specimen with **dense growth and more flowering points. Why and When to Prune**

Though Christmas Cactus plants are naturally elegant in their cascading form, pruning provides both **functional and aesthetic benefits**. Understanding the reasons behind this process will help you prune with confidence, while the correct timing ensures minimal stress to the plant and maximum benefit.

Why You Should Prune Your Christmas Cactus

1. **Encourage Fuller, Bushier Growth**
   Pruning stimulates new growth at the base of the trimmed segments. This results in **denser branching**, more terminal ends, and a better chance for increased bud and flower production.
2. **Remove Damaged or Aged Segments**
   Over time, older segments can become woody, wrinkled, or unproductive. Pruning these back encourages the plant to divert energy to newer, healthier stems.

3. **Control Size and Shape**
   While cascading plants are beautiful, they can become unwieldy or one-sided. Pruning helps shape the plant into a **balanced, symmetrical form** that suits hanging baskets, tabletop pots, or decorative displays.
4. **Rejuvenate a Neglected or Leggy Plant**
   A plant that has grown tall and thin with long, sparsely segmented arms can be revitalized with strategic pruning. It reestablishes a compact framework and improves future bloom potential.
5. **Prevent Overcrowding and Improve Air Circulation**
   Dense plants may trap moisture and limit airflow between segments, increasing the risk of fungal infections. Thinning out congested areas promotes plant health.

When to Prune Your Christmas Cactus

- **Best time to prune: Late winter to early spring**, after the plant has completed its blooming cycle and entered a rest period. This is when the plant is less vulnerable to shock and has time to heal and grow before the next blooming season.
- **Avoid pruning**:
  o **During bud formation (fall)**: Can disrupt the bloom cycle.
  o **During active flowering (winter)**: May cause premature bud drop.
  o **Immediately after repotting**: Let the plant stabilize before pruning.

Seasonal Timing Overview

- **Late Winter/Early Spring**: Ideal for shaping, thinning, and size control.
- **Summer**: Light trimming can be done to manage growth or propagate.
- **Fall**: Avoid pruning as this is the bloom initiation phase.

By pruning at the right time and for the right reasons, you'll keep your Christmas Cactus vibrant, manageable, and blooming at its best.

How to Prune Without Damaging the Plant

Pruning may seem intimidating, especially when you're dealing with a well-established or heirloom plant. However, Christmas Cactus responds remarkably well to trimming—**provided it's done with care, cleanliness, and precision.**

1. Tools You'll Need

- **Clean, sharp scissors or pruning shears**
- **Rubbing alcohol or hydrogen peroxide** for sterilizing
- **Optional: gloves** (though not necessary since the plant is non-toxic and non-spiny)

2. Sterilize Your Tools

Always sterilize your tools before cutting to prevent the spread of disease. Wipe blades with rubbing alcohol

84

between cuts if working with a plant that shows signs of disease or decay.

3. Identify Your Cutting Points

Each stem of a Christmas Cactus consists of multiple **flattened segments**, or *cladodes*, connected end to end. These segments naturally break apart at the joints, which is where you should cut.

* Cut **between segments**, never through the middle of one.
* Hold the segment just above the joint and gently **twist** or use scissors to make a clean break.
* Avoid cutting more than **one-third** of the plant at a time to prevent stress.

4. Where and How Much to Cut

* For **shaping**: Cut longer stems back by **2–3 segments** to maintain form.
* For **revitalizing**: Remove any thin, wrinkled, discolored, or woody stems.
* For **thinning**: Trim overly dense clusters to improve airflow.
* For **symmetry**: Identify uneven areas and reduce growth on the longer side to balance the plant.

5. Aftercare Following Pruning

* Do **not water immediately** after pruning—give the wounds 1–2 days to callus over.
* Return the plant to its normal location with bright, indirect light.

- Resume regular watering after 3–5 days and avoid feeding for 2 weeks to allow healing.

By using clean techniques and respecting the plant's natural growth pattern, you'll ensure quick recovery and encourage robust new growth.

Promoting Fuller Growth through Trimming

The cascading stems of a Christmas Cactus can create a beautiful silhouette, but without intervention, the plant may develop long, stringy branches with very few side shoots. Regular trimming, even in small amounts, is the key to **creating a lush, bushy plant** full of life and flowers.

1. Why Fuller Growth Matters

- More branches = more growing tips
- More tips = more potential flower sites
- Fuller appearance enhances aesthetic value and bloom coverage

2. How Trimming Stimulates New Branching
When a segment is removed, the plant's energy is redirected to the nearest **areole**, or growth node. This encourages the development of:

- **One or more new segments** near the cut
- **Lateral branching**, rather than extended vertical growth
- **Compact growth habits** in previously leggy stems

3. Techniques to Promote Density

- **Tip pruning**: Remove just the end segment on each branch—encourages the plant to fork and branch at that point.
- **Staggered trimming**: Prune some stems one year, others the next to maintain continuous growth and flowering.
- **Pinching back**: Use your fingers to gently twist off small segments instead of cutting. This simulates natural breakage and can stimulate vigorous response.

4. Recovery and Growth Expectations

- New growth typically emerges **within 2 to 6 weeks** post-pruning.
- Fertilize lightly about a month after pruning to support tissue regeneration.
- Regular trimming once a year is generally sufficient for mature plants.

Over time, even a sparse or older cactus can be rejuvenated into a **dense, symmetrical showpiece** by applying these techniques with patience and consistency.

Controlling Size and Direction

A common challenge with mature Christmas Cactus plants is their **size and directional sprawl**. While their natural growth habit is semi-trailing, without intervention, they can become **unbalanced, top-heavy, or awkwardly shaped**—especially in small living spaces or indoor displays.

1. Controlling Size Through Selective Pruning

- Focus on **outermost branches** that have grown too long.
- Remove segments where stems are **dragging, flopping, or bending under their weight.**
- Cut back up to **25% of the total stem length,** ideally just above a healthy segment that shows signs of branching.

2. Managing Vertical vs. Horizontal Growth

- If stems are growing straight up with no lateral spread, prune to encourage **side shoots**.
- For overly downward or sprawling stems, prune back to promote **upward-facing branches** from nodes near the base.

3. Shaping the Plant for Display

- **Hanging baskets**: Encourage even, cascading growth by rotating the pot regularly and trimming any overly dominant branches.
- **Tabletop containers**: Shape into a dome or fountain form by cutting back long side stems and encouraging upward growth near the center.

4. Tips for Directional Control

- Use pruning combined with **strategic lighting** to guide growth—plants will lean toward the light source.
- **Rotate the pot every 1–2 weeks** to promote balanced growth and even blooming.

By mastering pruning as a form of sculpting, you can train your plant to **fit its space, highlight its best features**, and create a beautiful display that blooms exactly where and how you want it to.

Using Pruned Pieces for Propagation

One of the great joys of growing Christmas Cactus is that **every segment you remove can become a new plant**. Propagation through pruning not only prevents waste but also allows you to:

- Expand your collection
- Share cuttings with friends and family
- Preserve legacy plants by creating backups

1. Selecting Cuttings for Propagation

- Choose healthy, firm segments that are **at least 2 to 4 segments long**.
- Avoid using damaged, diseased, or overly woody material.
- The ideal cutting has **a clean break at the joint**, is free of rot, and has no flower buds (which divert energy).

2. Preparing Cuttings

- Let the cuttings **dry for 24–48 hours** until the ends form a callus. This helps prevent rot when planted.
- Place them in a **bright but indirect light** location during this drying period.

3. Rooting Medium

- Use a light, well-draining mix such as:
  o 50% cactus soil + 50% perlite
  o Alternatively, a mix of peat, sand, and perlite
- Moisten the medium slightly before inserting cuttings.

4. Planting the Cuttings

- Insert each cutting about **1 inch deep**, ensuring at least one segment is above the soil.
- Keep the pot in a warm, bright spot (65–75°F) with indirect light.
- Mist lightly or water sparingly until roots form— typically within **3 to 6 weeks**.

5. Post-Rooting Care

- After root development, begin watering more regularly.
- Transplant to a permanent pot once new growth is visible.
- Resume light fertilization after 2–3 months.

6. Tips for Successful Propagation

- Label your cuttings if experimenting with different colors or hybrids.
- Propagate multiple cuttings together in one pot for a bushier starter plant.
- Spring is the best season to root cuttings, aligning with the plant's natural growth cycle.

Through propagation, every pruning session becomes an opportunity to multiply beauty, **share heirlooms**, and ensure your Christmas Cactus lives on for generations.

Pruning a Christmas Cactus isn't just about aesthetics—it's about nurturing the plant's full potential. From **stimulating fresh growth, controlling shape**, and **encouraging more flowers**, to **producing new plants** through propagation, thoughtful trimming gives you control over both the plant's structure and its seasonal performance.

When done with the right timing, tools, and technique, pruning can revitalize an aging plant, correct years of imbalance, and turn a modest cactus into a **stunning centerpiece** that blooms in glorious color every holiday season. Whether your goal is to shape, shrink, multiply, or simply strengthen, pruning is the powerful, underrated skill every Christmas Cactus grower should master.

CHAPTER FOUR

PROPAGATION METHODS EXPLAINED

The beauty of the Christmas Cactus (*Schlumbergera* ×
   buckleyi) extends far beyond its holiday blooms. One of
   its most endearing qualities is how easily it can be
   shared. With just a single segment, you can grow an
   entirely new plant—a living gift, a clone of a beloved
   specimen, or simply an expansion of your own indoor
   garden.

Unlike many houseplants that require specialized
   techniques, propagating Christmas Cactus is **simple,
   reliable, and rewarding** when done correctly. This
   chapter breaks down the two most popular
   propagation techniques—soil and water rooting—
   along with a comprehensive step-by-step guide and
   best practices for caring for new plants during their
   early stages of life.

Propagating by Stem Cuttings

Stem cutting is by far the most common and effective
   method of propagating Christmas Cactus. This method
   leverages the plant's natural ability to regenerate from
   cladodes, or the flattened stem segments that make up
   its branching structure. These segments contain nodes

that can develop into roots and eventually grow into a full plant.

Why Stem Cuttings Work

Christmas Cactus has evolved as an **epiphyte,** growing on trees and absorbing moisture from the air and rain. Its stems are built to store water and nutrients, and its segmented design allows for easy breakage and regrowth—an evolutionary adaptation that makes **vegetative propagation particularly efficient**.

Advantages of Propagation by Stem Cuttings

- High success rate
- Requires minimal equipment or expertise
- Produces genetically identical offspring
- Fast rooting time under proper conditions
- Encourages plant sharing, gift-giving, and collection expansion

Ideal Cuttings

- Each cutting should consist of **2 to 4 healthy segments**
- The segments should be **firm, green, and blemish-free**
- Avoid pieces with flower buds, as they can divert energy from root development
- Segments from the **middle or upper sections** of the plant tend to root faster than very old or woody stems

Propagation through cuttings can be done in **soil or water**, each with its own advantages and challenges, which we'll now explore.

Soil vs. Water Rooting Techniques

Both soil and water can be used to root Christmas Cactus cuttings, but the best choice depends on your environment, preference, and experience level. Each method has its own timeline, pros, and risks.

Soil Rooting Method

This is the **preferred method** among seasoned growers and more closely mimics the plant's natural growth conditions.

Advantages

- Less risk of transplant shock
- Roots develop in the medium they'll continue growing in
- Better oxygen exchange for roots
- Easier to maintain humidity balance

Steps Summary

- Let the cuttings callus for 24–48 hours
- Insert into well-draining cactus mix
- Mist lightly or water sparingly
- Place in bright, indirect light
- Roots usually form in 2 to 4 weeks

94

Challenges

- Harder to observe root progress without disturbing the plant
- Risk of overwatering if the medium is too dense

Water Rooting Method

This method is favored by beginners and those who want visual confirmation of root development.

Advantages

- Easy to monitor root growth
- High success rate with clean water and good hygiene
- Useful for those lacking cactus soil or propagation trays

Steps Summary

- Let cuttings callus
- Place lower segment tip in clean water (only the base submerged)
- Use clear container in indirect light
- Change water every 3 days
- Transplant to soil when roots are 1–2 inches long

Challenges

- Risk of stem rot if submerged too deeply
- Roots may be weaker or slower to adjust after transplant
- Requires transition to soil at the right moment to avoid stunted growth

Which Should You Choose?

- **For robust long-term growth**: Start in soil
- **For ease and observation**: Try water rooting, especially for your first attempt

Ultimately, both methods can lead to strong, healthy plants when executed with attention to detail and proper aftercare.

When to Start Propagation for Best Results

Timing plays a major role in the success of propagation. Although Christmas Cactus can technically be propagated year-round indoors, certain windows provide **faster rooting and lower stress** on the plant.

Best Season: Late Spring to Early Summer

- The plant is in its **active growth phase**, which means it's metabolically primed for regeneration.
- Warmer temperatures and increased light stimulate root development.
- The parent plant has recovered from blooming and pruning, making it ideal for cuttings.

Other Viable Windows

- **Early fall**: If conditions are warm and consistent, cuttings may root before dormancy.
- **Avoid late fall to early winter**, especially during the blooming period, as the plant's energy is focused on flowering, not regeneration.

Other Factors That Influence Timing

- **Humidity**: Higher indoor humidity supports faster rooting.
- **Day length**: More light encourages metabolic activity and photosynthesis, aiding root development.
- **Plant health**: Never propagate from a stressed or diseased plant.

Signs It's a Good Time to Propagate

- Your plant has just been pruned
- You're repotting and find healthy segments that can be salvaged
- You have access to a healthy donor plant with vigorous growth

Choosing the right time to propagate can mean the difference between a struggling cutting and a thriving new plant.

Step-by-Step Propagation Guide

Whether you choose water or soil as your rooting medium, following a step-by-step approach will maximize your success rate. Below is a detailed guide to propagating a Christmas Cactus from start to finish.

Step 1: Select the Right Cutting

- Choose a stem with **2 to 4 healthy, firm segments**
- Avoid pieces with flower buds or signs of rot
- Snip or gently twist at the natural joint between segments

97

Step 2: Let the Cutting Callus

- Place the cuttings on a **paper towel or plate** in a bright, dry place
- Allow the cut ends to dry and form a **callus** (typically 24–48 hours)
- This reduces the risk of rot when planted or submerged

Step 3A: Rooting in Soil

1. Prepare a small pot with a **well-draining mix** (cactus mix + perlite or sand)
2. Moisten the soil slightly—**damp, not wet**
3. Insert the base of the cutting about 1 inch deep
4. Gently firm the soil around it to hold it upright
5. Place the pot in **bright, indirect light**
6. Mist lightly every few days until roots form
7. Avoid direct sun, overwatering, or feeding during this phase

Step 3B: Rooting in Water

1. Fill a small, clean jar or cup with **filtered or distilled water**
2. Submerge only the **bottom 1/4 inch** of the cutting
3. Prop the segment so it remains upright
4. Place in a warm spot with **indirect sunlight**
5. Change the water every **2–3 days** to prevent stagnation
6. Once roots are **1–2 inches long**, transplant to soil

Step 4: Transitioning to Soil (for Water-Rooted Plants)

1. Prepare a pot with fresh cactus soil

2. Water lightly and make a small hole
3. Gently place the rooted cutting in the soil
4. Do not compact the soil too much
5. Wait 3–5 days before the next watering to allow root acclimation

Step 5: Monitor and Support New Growth

- Expect new segment growth within **4–8 weeks**
- Resume feeding after 8–10 weeks with diluted cactus fertilizer
- Re-pot to a slightly larger container once the plant has outgrown its starter pot

By following this propagation blueprint, you'll maximize root success and ensure strong starts for your baby Christmas Cactus plants.

Caring for Baby Christmas Cactus Plants

Once your cuttings have rooted, the real work begins. These young plants require **different care** than mature specimens—especially in their first few months. The transition from cutting to self-sustaining plant can be delicate, so monitoring and gradual adjustments are key.

1. Light Requirements

- Provide **bright, indirect light**
- Avoid full sun exposure for the first 2–3 months
- Gradually acclimate the plant to stronger light as it matures

2. Watering Guidelines

- Keep the soil **slightly moist,** not wet
- Water thoroughly only when the **top inch** is dry
- Avoid frequent misting that can encourage mold near the stem base

3. Humidity and Temperature

- Ideal temperature range: **65°F to 75°F (18°C to 24°C)**
- Moderate to high humidity (40–60%) helps young plants establish
- Use humidity trays or grouped plants to improve local conditions

4. Feeding Young Plants

- Begin feeding only **8 to 10 weeks** after rooting
- Use a **half-strength balanced fertilizer** once a month
- Avoid high-nitrogen formulas to prevent spindly growth

5. Growth and Repotting

- New segments should begin forming within 6–10 weeks
- Don't rush to transplant—wait until the roots are well-established
- When repotting, choose a pot **just 1 inch larger** than the current one

6. Common Issues in Young Plants

- **Yellowing segments**: Usually due to overwatering or poor drainage
- **Wilting**: Can indicate either drought or rot—check the soil
- **No growth after several months**: Likely due to low light or temperature stress

7. Gradual Integration into Regular Care

- By month 3 or 4, your baby cactus can be moved into a regular care routine
- Resume seasonal watering, light adjustments, and eventual pruning
- The plant should bloom after **12 to 18 months**, depending on environmental conditions and size

Successfully nurturing propagated Christmas Cactus plants from segment to flowering adult is a gratifying experience. With time and care, they'll not only grow—they'll thrive.

Propagation is more than a horticultural technique—it's a way to **preserve plant heritage, multiply beauty**, and **share joy**. The Christmas Cactus makes propagation easy, forgiving, and deeply rewarding. Whether you're rooting a sentimental segment from a grandmother's heirloom plant or simply multiplying your own collection, the methods explored in this chapter provide a clear, confident path.

By understanding the difference between water and soil techniques, choosing the right season, following precise steps, and giving your baby plants the care they deserve, you can turn every pruning session into an opportunity for growth—both for your plants and your skill as a gardener.

PEST AND DISEASE PREVENTION

No matter how carefully you tend to your Christmas Cactus (*Schlumbergera* × *buckleyi*), the possibility of pest infestations or disease outbreaks remains a constant threat. These issues can arise suddenly, and if left unchecked, can compromise the health of even the most vigorous plant. Unlike some houseplants, Christmas Cactus is relatively resilient—but it is not immune. Pests can feed on sap, weaken stems, and open the door to secondary infections, while fungal and bacterial diseases can rot roots, blacken tissue, and halt blooming altogether.

Fortunately, with proper care, early detection, and a solid prevention routine, most issues can be avoided or corrected before they become fatal. This chapter explores the most common pests and pathogens affecting Christmas Cactus, the signs to look for, a full overview of both natural and chemical treatment methods, best practices for maintaining a clean growing environment, and how to make difficult decisions when it's time to quarantine or discard a plant for the health of the others.

Common Pests: Mealybugs, Spider Mites, and More

Christmas Cactus is not a magnet for pests, but when infestations do occur, they often involve **sap-feeding insects** that are attracted to soft, moisture-rich stem segments. These pests can multiply quickly and are often introduced via new plants, contaminated tools, or close contact with infected greenery.

1. Mealybugs

One of the most frequent pests seen on Christmas Cactus.

- **Identification**: Small, white, cottony masses usually clustered in stem joints or along veins.
- **Behavior**: Suck plant sap, weakening the plant and leading to yellowing or wilting.
- **Signs**:
  o Sticky honeydew on the surface
  o Presence of ants (which farm mealybugs for honeydew)
  o Distorted or shrunken segments

2. Spider Mites

Tiny arachnids barely visible to the naked eye.

- **Identification**: Fine webbing between stem segments, often near the tips or joints.
- **Behavior**: Feed by piercing plant cells and sucking out contents.
- **Signs**:
  o Silvery stippling on stem surfaces
  o Dull, rough patches on segments
  o Dry or thinning growth near the top

3. Fungus Gnats

These are small, black flying insects whose larvae feed on roots and decaying matter.

- **Identification**: Adults resemble tiny black mosquitoes hovering near the soil.
- **Behavior**: Lay eggs in moist soil; larvae feed on roots and organic material.
- **Signs**:
  o Wilting or yellowing despite moist soil
  o Slow growth in younger plants
  o Frequent sightings of adults near pots

4. Scale Insects

Hard- or soft-bodied insects that attach to stems and segments.

- **Identification**: Small, dome-shaped brown or tan bumps stuck to plant surfaces.
- **Behavior**: Feed on sap, often unnoticed until damage is advanced.
- **Signs**:
  o Yellow halos around feeding sites
  o Waxy coating or honeydew residue
  o Plant weakening without visible movement

5. Aphids

Though rare on Christmas Cactus, they can appear on new growth or flower buds.

- **Identification**: Soft-bodied green, black, or white insects, usually in clusters.
- **Behavior**: Feed on tender tissues, especially flower buds.
- **Signs**:
  o Curled or misshapen new segments
  o Sticky residue and black sooty mold
  o Bud drop or bloom deformity

Quick identification and isolation of the affected plant can prevent pests from spreading to others nearby.

Identifying Fungal and Bacterial Infections

Beyond pests, Christmas Cactus is vulnerable to a variety of **fungal and bacterial pathogens**, especially in humid or overwatered conditions. These diseases are often harder to spot and can become systemic if not addressed quickly.

1. Root Rot (Fungal – *Pythium*, *Phytophthora*)

- **Cause**: Poor drainage, constant moisture, or infected soil.
- **Symptoms**:
  o Soft, blackened roots that smell foul
  o Wilted appearance despite moist soil
  o Mushy base of stem segments
- **Action**:
  o Remove from pot, prune affected roots
  o Repot in dry, sterile, well-draining soil

o   Reduce watering frequency

2. Stem Rot (Fungal/Bacterial)

- **Cause**: Entry through wounds or prolonged dampness at the soil line.
- **Symptoms**:
o   Black or brown lesions on lower stems
o   Soft, watery tissue around the base
o   Segments fall off with little resistance
- **Action**:
o   Prune infected segments
o   Sterilize tools between cuts
o   Discard severely affected specimens

3. Botrytis Blight (Fungal – *Botrytis cinerea*)

- **Cause**: High humidity and poor airflow.
- **Symptoms**:
o   Grayish mold on flowers or joints
o   Water-soaked patches on stems
o   Premature flower or bud drop
- **Action**:
o   Improve ventilation
o   Remove affected flowers or parts
o   Apply antifungal spray if necessary

4. Bacterial Soft Rot (*Erwinia* species)

- **Cause**: Enters through damaged tissue.
- **Symptoms**:
o   Slime-like ooze
o   Foul odor
o   Rapid collapse of tissue

- **Action**:
  o Discard entire plant
  o Clean area thoroughly
  o Avoid reusing soil or pot

Early detection is vital. Regular inspection of stem joints, soil surface, and root systems during repotting can help catch these issues before they spread.

Natural and Chemical Treatment Options

When pests or diseases appear, acting fast with the correct treatment method can make the difference between recovery and loss. Fortunately, there are **both natural and chemical options** depending on the severity and personal preference.

Natural Treatments

Ideal for minor infestations or routine prevention.

1. Neem Oil Spray

- Broad-spectrum insecticide and fungicide
- Mix 1–2 teaspoons per quart of water with a few drops of dish soap
- Apply weekly to all plant surfaces
- Effective against mealybugs, aphids, mites

2. Insecticidal Soap

- Kills soft-bodied insects on contact

- Use commercial products or mix 1 tablespoon of mild liquid soap with 1 quart water
- Spray thoroughly but avoid direct sun after application

3. Hydrogen Peroxide Drench

- 3% hydrogen peroxide solution can kill fungus gnat larvae in soil
- Mix 1 part peroxide with 4 parts water
- Water the soil thoroughly once, not repeatedly

4. Cinnamon or Sulfur Powder

- Acts as a natural antifungal
- Dust affected areas or sprinkle on soil surface after pruning

5. Isopropyl Alcohol (70%)

- Use a cotton swab to remove individual mealybugs or scale insects
- Do not spray directly on large areas without testing first

Chemical Treatments

Best used for moderate to severe infestations or infections.

1. Systemic Insecticides

- Absorbed by the plant and kills sap-sucking insects from within
- Available as granules or liquid concentrates
- Use only as directed and not during flowering

2. Fungicides

- Copper-based sprays or biofungicides like Bacillus subtilis
- Use for blight, rot, and mildew issues
- Apply during cool, dry times of day and avoid spraying buds

3. Soil Sterilizers

- Use only as a last resort or before replanting in infested soil
- Can kill beneficial microbes, so recondition soil afterward

Important Tips

- Always test treatments on a small section before widespread use
- Use personal protection when applying chemical controls
- Never mix treatments without clear guidance

When possible, **start with natural methods** and escalate to chemical solutions only if the problem persists or worsens.

Keeping a Clean Growing Environment

The best defense against pests and disease is **preventative care**. A clean, well-maintained growing environment ensures that your Christmas Cactus has the best chance to grow, bloom, and remain healthy over time.

1. Sanitize Tools and Containers

- Sterilize scissors, pots, and trays before use
- Wash hands before handling multiple plants
- Avoid reusing soil unless properly sterilized

2. Quarantine New Plants

- Isolate new acquisitions for 2–3 weeks
- Monitor for insects, mold, or stress signs
- Keep separate from healthy, established plants

3. Practice Good Watering Habits

- Water only when the soil is dry to the touch
- Avoid splashing stems or pooling water around the base
- Use containers with proper drainage holes

4. Optimize Air Circulation

- Keep space between plants to prevent humidity buildup
- Use a small fan in stagnant corners or greenhouse shelves
- Rotate plants periodically for even airflow and light exposure

5. Inspect Regularly

- Examine stem joints, leaf undersides, and soil weekly
- Look for pests, sticky residue, mold, and signs of discoloration
- Act at the first sign of trouble—early intervention is key

6. Clean Surroundings

- Remove dead flowers or leaves from the soil surface
- Keep shelves, windowsills, and saucers dry and clean
- Disinfect grow trays between seasons

Prevention doesn't require expensive equipment—just **consistency, observation, and hygiene**.

When to Quarantine or Discard a Plant

Despite your best efforts, there may come a time when an infected or infested plant becomes too risky to keep among your healthy collection. Knowing **when to isolate** or **remove a plant permanently** is essential for protecting the others.

1. When to Quarantine

- Any plant showing **unidentified symptoms**
- A newly purchased or gifted plant
- A plant recently treated for pests or disease
- A plant recovering from shock, root rot, or severe pruning

Isolation Guidelines

111

- Place in a separate room with similar light and temperature
- Avoid sharing tools, watering cans, or misting equipment
- Monitor daily for progress or worsening

2. When to Discard

- Systemic infections such as bacterial soft rot that cannot be contained
- Plants with extensive root or stem rot
- Recurrent pest infestations that spread despite treatment
- Cases where more than 50% of the plant is damaged or necrotic

Disposal Tips

- Double-bag and seal the plant before discarding
- Do not compost diseased material
- Sterilize the pot and tools used with a bleach solution (1:9 ratio)

3. Emotional Consideration
If the plant is a sentimental gift or family heirloom:

- Consider salvaging healthy cuttings and starting anew
- Share cuttings with others as a legacy if saving the whole plant isn't possible

Being proactive and decisive about plant health ultimately benefits the entire collection—and saves time, energy, and heartache in the long run.

Pest and disease prevention is not a one-time task—it is a **continuous part of responsible plant care**. By staying vigilant, maintaining cleanliness, and responding quickly to the first signs of trouble, you'll ensure your Christmas Cactus remains strong, vibrant, and bloom-ready each year.

From mealybugs to bacterial rot, the threats are real—but so are the solutions. With the right combination of natural defenses, smart growing practices, and when necessary, targeted treatments, you can keep your plants healthy and your indoor garden flourishing. Prevention, after all, is the best form of protection.

TROUBLESHOOTING COMMON PROBLEMS

No matter how careful or experienced a grower is, there will inevitably come a time when a Christmas Cactus doesn't look its best. Leaves droop, buds drop, colors change, or growth stalls altogether. These symptoms often seem sudden but are usually the result of **underlying care issues**, environmental imbalances, or delayed stress responses. Thankfully, most problems with Christmas Cactus can be reversed when diagnosed correctly and addressed early.

Dropping Buds and Flowers

Few things are more disappointing than seeing flower buds form, only to watch them fall off before they open.

113

Bud and flower drop is a common frustration for Christmas Cactus growers and is usually triggered by sudden changes in the plant's environment during the **critical blooming phase**.

1. Causes of Bud Drop

- **Sudden Environmental Change**
  - Moving the plant once buds have formed can shock the system.
  - Changes in location, temperature, or light disrupt the blooming cycle.
- **Overwatering or Underwatering**
  - Waterlogged roots stress the plant, causing buds to abort.
  - Allowing the plant to dry out too much also dehydrates developing buds.
- **Temperature Extremes**
  - Exposure to heat sources, drafts, or cold windows can cause buds to detach.
  - Ideal temperatures during budding range from **60°F to 70°F (15°C to 21°C)**.
- **Low Humidity**
  - Dry indoor air, especially in winter, can cause delicate buds to wither and fall.
- **Nutrient Imbalance**
  - Excess nitrogen during the pre-bloom phase favors foliage over flowers.
  - Insufficient phosphorus and potassium hinder bud retention.

2. Causes of Flower Drop

- **Natural Aging**

114

- o Flowers typically last 5 to 10 days and then drop naturally.
- **Physical Disturbance**
- o Touching or brushing against flowers can cause them to fall prematurely.
- **Improper Watering During Bloom**
- o Either overwatering or letting the plant dry out can cause open blooms to fall.

3. Solutions and Prevention

- Avoid moving the plant during the bud or bloom phase.
- Keep conditions stable—consistent light, temperature, and watering.
- Water when the top inch of soil feels dry but never allow complete dehydration.
- Increase humidity using trays or room humidifiers during bloom.
- Use a balanced fertilizer prior to bud formation, but **stop feeding once buds appear**.

Catching and correcting these issues early will allow the plant to retain and open its buds successfully, leading to a vibrant and extended bloom period.

Wilted or Limp Leaves

One of the most visually alarming problems for Christmas Cactus growers is when the segments suddenly appear **droopy, soft, or limp**. This can be due to several factors, including **water stress, root damage, or environmental shock**.

115

1. Overwatering

- **Symptoms**:
  o Leaves feel mushy and soft, especially near the base.
  o Soil stays wet for long periods.
  o May be accompanied by yellowing or blackened stems.
- **Cause**:
  o Waterlogged soil prevents oxygen from reaching roots, leading to root rot.
  o Damaged roots can no longer absorb water, causing above-ground wilting.
- **Solution**:
  o Stop watering immediately.
  o Remove the plant from its pot, inspect and trim away black or mushy roots.
  o Repot in fresh, well-draining cactus mix.
  o Water sparingly until the plant stabilizes.

2. Underwatering

- **Symptoms**:
  o Leaves are thin, wrinkled, or drooping.
  o Soil is completely dry and pulling away from the pot edges.
- **Cause**:
  o Lack of water leads to dehydration and collapsed cell walls in the stems.
- **Solution**:
  o Water thoroughly until excess drains out.
  o Resume consistent watering—typically every 7–10 days during active growth.
  o Avoid allowing the soil to dry out entirely between waterings.

3. Sudden Temperature Drop

- **Symptoms:**
  - o Leaves droop or collapse without signs of dehydration.
  - o May occur after a cold night or near a drafty window.
- **Solution:**
  - o Move the plant to a warmer location with consistent temperatures.
  - o Avoid exposure to temperatures below 50°F (10°C).

4. Root or Stem Disease

- **Symptoms:**
  - o Persistent wilting despite correct watering.
  - o Foul odor from soil or base of plant.
- **Solution:**
  - o Uproot and inspect roots for signs of rot or fungal infection.
  - o Prune affected areas, sterilize pot, and repot in dry, clean soil.

Wilting is almost always a sign of root function failure. Addressing the underlying cause quickly can save the plant from systemic decline.

Yellowing or Browning Segments

Discoloration in the otherwise rich green segments of the Christmas Cactus is a sign of **stress, nutrient imbalance, or disease**. The location, pattern, and progression of the color change offer valuable diagnostic clues.

1. Yellowing Segments

117

- **Overwatering**
- Yellowing at the base segments, especially combined with soggy soil, indicates root suffocation.
- **Underwatering**
- Uniform yellowing across the plant due to prolonged dryness.
- **Nutrient Deficiency**
- **Nitrogen deficiency** causes pale or yellow foliage.
- Lack of magnesium or iron may result in **interveinal chlorosis**—yellowing between the veins.
- **Excess Light**
- Direct sunlight causes yellowing and eventual bleaching.

2. Browning Segments

- **Sunburn**
- Brown, dry patches on segments exposed to hot, direct sunlight.
- Especially common in plants moved outside without acclimation.
- **Physical Damage**
- Bruising or crushing can cause brown scabs or lesions.
- **Fungal Infection**
- Dark brown spots or lesions may spread—typically wet or sunken.
- Often requires antifungal treatment and removal of affected parts.

3. Environmental Shock

- Transplanting, repotting, or moving the plant can lead to short-term discoloration.

Corrective Measures

- Adjust watering practices to the plant's seasonal needs.
- Move the plant to a location with bright, **indirect light**.
- Test and balance soil pH and nutrient content.
- Apply a gentle, diluted fertilizer if deficiencies are suspected.
- Remove any infected or sunburned segments with sterilized scissors.

Observing how and where the discoloration occurs will help isolate the root cause and guide the appropriate fix.

Lack of Growth or Sparse Blooming

A Christmas Cactus that remains alive but shows **little to no growth or flowering** can still be healthy but lacking proper environmental stimulation. These conditions often relate to **light, feeding, pot space, or seasonal cycle misalignment**.

1. Inadequate Light

- Plants kept in low-light locations may survive but show:
  o No new segment development
  o Stretched or spindly growth
  o Lack of flowering even during bloom season
- **Solution:**
  o Move to a location with **bright, indirect light** (east- or north-facing window).
  o Avoid deep interior spaces with little natural light.

2. Overly Root-Bound

- While Christmas Cactus prefers to be slightly root-bound, extreme crowding can stunt growth.
- **Symptoms**:
- o Roots circling inside the pot
- o Soil dries out too quickly
- o Stunted new segment formation
- **Solution**:
- o Repot every 3–4 years into a container only slightly larger (1–2 inches wider).
- o Refresh soil and inspect roots during transplant.

3. Improper Fertilization

- Lack of key nutrients will limit the plant's ability to expand or bloom.
- Over-fertilizing, especially with high nitrogen, can favor green growth but suppress flowering.
- **Solution**:
- o Use a **balanced fertilizer** in spring and summer.
- o Switch to a **low-nitrogen, high-phosphorus** formula in late summer to encourage blooming.

4. No Dormancy Period

- Failure to induce a **short-day and cool-night period** in the fall will prevent bud initiation.
- **Solution**:
- o Provide at least **12–14 hours of darkness** daily for 4–6 weeks in autumn.

o   Drop nighttime temperatures to **50–55°F (10–13°C)** to mimic natural dormancy.

With patience and the right adjustments, most underperforming Christmas Cactus plants can be brought back into active growth and regular bloom cycles.

Diagnosing Problems by Symptoms

Recognizing **specific symptoms and their patterns** is the fastest route to diagnosing the cause of any problem. Below is a quick reference chart and explanation of how to interpret what your plant is telling you.

Symptom: Bud Drop

- **Likely Causes**:
o   Drafts or sudden movement
o   Over- or underwatering
o   Low humidity
o   Night lighting interruptions
- **Solution**:
o   Stabilize conditions and avoid disruptions

Symptom: Wilting or Limp Segments

- **Likely Causes**:
o   Root rot (overwatering)
o   Dehydration
o   Cold exposure
- **Solution**:

o Inspect roots, adjust watering, and maintain stable temps

Symptom: Yellowing

- **Likely Causes:**
o Water imbalance
o Nutrient deficiency
o Sun stress
- **Solution:**
o Test and adjust watering, feed with diluted balanced fertilizer, move to indirect light

Symptom: Brown Spots

- **Likely Causes:**
o Sunburn
o Physical damage
o Fungal infection
- **Solution:**
o Prune affected areas, apply antifungal if spreading

Symptom: No Growth

- **Likely Causes:**
o Low light
o Root crowding
o Dormancy not broken
- **Solution:**
o Relocate, repot, and encourage growth with proper feeding

Symptom: No Blooms

- **Likely Causes**:
  - No dark/cool period
  - Improper feeding
  - Excess nitrogen
- **Solution**:
  - Initiate 4–6 week dormancy with dark/cool conditions, then return to bright light

This symptom-based approach helps eliminate guesswork and empowers growers to respond quickly and effectively to changes in plant behavior.

Problems are inevitable in any plant care journey—but for the Christmas Cactus, they are rarely irreversible. With its forgiving nature and resilience, this plant rewards observation and thoughtful intervention. Whether it's drooping segments, dropped buds, or stubborn growth, nearly every issue has a clear cause and a practical solution.

By learning to **read the signs**, make timely adjustments, and avoid overcorrection, growers can turn setbacks into learning experiences. With patience, consistent care, and proper troubleshooting techniques, your Christmas Cactus can return to vibrant health—and resume blooming with holiday magic year after year.

CHAPTER FIVE

YOUR OUTDOOR GROWING TIPS

The Christmas Cactus (Schlumbergera × buckleyi), a beloved houseplant known for its brilliant holiday blooms, is often assumed to be strictly an indoor species. This assumption stems from its origins in Brazil's shaded rainforests and its reputation for disliking frost. However, under the right conditions and with proper care, Christmas Cactus can thrive outdoors and even flourish with increased vigor and blooming potential.

Can Christmas Cactus Thrive Outdoors?

The answer is yes—**with proper environmental conditions and management**, Christmas Cactus can indeed grow well outdoors. In fact, many gardeners find that outdoor exposure enhances the plant's overall health and blooming performance.

1. Origin and Natural Habitats

The Christmas Cactus is a tropical epiphyte native to the coastal mountains of southeastern Brazil. It naturally grows in humid forests, nestled in tree branches or rock crevices under a canopy of filtered sunlight. These natural conditions mimic outdoor environments more closely than the average dry, heated indoor space.

2. Outdoor Growing Zones

- Christmas Cactus can be **grown outdoors year-round** in **USDA Hardiness Zones 10 to 12**, where temperatures rarely drop below 40°F (4°C).
- In **Zones 9 and lower**, the plant can be grown outdoors only during warm months (spring through early fall) and must be **brought inside before frost.**
- The **ideal temperature range** for outdoor growth is **60°F to 85°F (15°C to 29°C)**, with high humidity and good airflow.

3. Benefits of Outdoor Growth

- **Improved Air Circulation**: Prevents stagnant conditions and fungal buildup.
- **Natural Light Cycles**: Helps trigger blooming at the right time of year.
- **Increased Humidity**: Especially in shaded garden areas, mimicking rainforest environments.
- **Enhanced Growth and Blooming**: Natural stress cycles and microclimate variations encourage the plant to flower more profusely.

While outdoor growth has clear advantages, it also introduces environmental challenges—especially exposure to temperature fluctuations, pests, and excessive sunlight. Understanding how to manage these risks is essential to outdoor success.

Choosing the Right Season and Spot

Successful outdoor cultivation hinges on knowing **when to move the plant outside** and **where to place it**.

Unlike many houseplants, Christmas Cactus responds dramatically to environmental changes, so careful planning is crucial.

1. Timing the Move Outdoors

- In temperate regions, **wait until nighttime temperatures remain consistently above 50°F (10°C)** before moving your plant outside—usually late spring.
- The **ideal time for outdoor placement** is **mid to late spring**, once all risk of frost has passed.
- Return the plant indoors in **early fall**, well before the first frost, to avoid cold damage and to begin the bloom initiation cycle.

2. Selecting the Ideal Location

The location you choose outdoors should mimic the **plant's native conditions**—shady, humid, and well-draining.

Characteristics of a good outdoor spot:

- **Filtered or dappled sunlight**: Under a porch, shade cloth, or tree canopy.
- **Sheltered from wind**: Christmas Cactus has fragile segments that snap in strong breezes.
- **Humidity-retaining microclimate**: Avoid overly dry spots like rock beds or exposed patios.
- **Elevated or potted placement**: Ensures drainage and minimizes contact with soil-borne pests.

3. Light Considerations

Christmas Cactus does not tolerate **direct afternoon sunlight**. Morning light or consistent shade with filtered rays throughout the day is best. Too much light can bleach or burn the plant's segments, while too little inhibits growth and blooming.

Protecting from Sunburn and Cold

Outdoor conditions can be harsh, especially during transitional seasons. To successfully acclimate your Christmas Cactus outdoors, you'll need to provide **layered protection** from both intense light and unexpected chills.

1. Preventing Sunburn

Sunburn in Christmas Cactus typically appears as **brown, leathery patches** or **faded bleached areas** on the flattened stem segments.

How to prevent it:

- **Acclimate gradually**: Introduce the plant to outdoor light slowly over 7–10 days.
- **Use filtered light**: Place under a tree or shade cloth that blocks at least 50% of direct sun.
- **Rotate regularly**: Turn the pot slightly each week to prevent uneven light exposure.

2. Shielding from Sudden Cold

Even in mild climates, summer nights can occasionally drop to dangerous temperatures.

Tips for cold protection:

- Monitor nighttime forecasts daily during spring and fall.
- Keep the plant on a **movable stand or rolling plant caddy** for quick indoor relocation.
- Use lightweight **frost blankets** if an unexpected cold front approaches.
- Avoid exposure to **drafty areas** or corners that trap cold air (such as courtyard alcoves).

3. Rain and Water Management

While Christmas Cactus enjoys humidity, **excessive rain or pooling water** can cause root rot.

- If left in a container outdoors, ensure it has **excellent drainage holes**.
- Avoid placing the plant where it will collect rainwater from gutters or roof runoff.
- Use **elevated stands** or saucers filled with gravel to prevent waterlogging.

Moving Between Indoors and Outdoors

Moving your plant between environments is more complex than simply carrying it outside. Christmas Cactus is sensitive to changes in **light, temperature,**

and humidity. Proper acclimation ensures a smooth transition and protects the plant from shock.

1. Spring Transition: Indoors to Outdoors

Steps for a safe transition:

- **Begin acclimation indoors**: Two weeks before the move, place the plant near an open window or vent.
- **Move to a shaded outdoor location** for 2–3 hours per day, increasing time gradually.
- Extend exposure by an hour each day until the plant remains outdoors full-time.
- Water carefully during this adjustment period to prevent dehydration or stress.

2. Fall Transition: Outdoors to Indoors

The reverse move is equally important for initiating the bloom cycle.

- **Begin acclimation in early fall** (when nights drop below 55°F or 13°C).
- Reduce watering to encourage a natural rest period.
- Move indoors gradually, starting with brief evening shelter and increasing indoor hours.
- Once inside, provide **12–14 hours of darkness and cool temperatures** (ideally 50–55°F or 10–13°C) to stimulate budding.

3. Transition Tips

- Clean leaves and inspect the plant thoroughly for pests before bringing it inside.

- Avoid placing the plant near **heat vents, fireplaces, or high-traffic zones**.
- Maintain **consistent humidity indoors** using trays, humidifiers, or misting.

The key to success is **predictability**—keep environmental changes minimal and gradual to prevent the plant from dropping buds or going dormant at the wrong time.

Outdoor Potting vs. Ground Planting

Should your Christmas Cactus live in a container or be planted directly into your garden? The answer depends on your location, climate, and intended long-term care.

1. Outdoor Container Growing

Most growers prefer container gardening for Christmas Cactus due to the control it provides.

Advantages:

- **Portability**: Easy to move indoors during cold weather or storms.
- **Controlled drainage**: Allows precise watering and soil management.
- **Flexibility**: Can be placed on porches, benches, plant stands, or tables.
- **Pest control**: Easier to monitor for infestations or root health.

Container considerations:

- Use a **breathable pot** (such as terracotta or unglazed ceramic) to allow air exchange.
- Ensure it has multiple drainage holes and is **not overly large** (cactus likes slightly snug roots).
- Place gravel or mesh at the base to prevent soil clogging and increase drainage.

2. In-Ground Planting

In frost-free regions, some gardeners choose to plant Christmas Cactus directly in the ground—particularly in tropical gardens or shaded beds.

Pros:

- **Natural habitat mimicry**: Soil layers, humidity, and organic matter mimic native conditions.
- **Space**: Allows the plant to expand without the limitations of a pot.
- **Aesthetic**: Can be integrated into rock gardens, shade beds, or under larger tropicals.

Cons:

- **Permanent exposure**: Cannot be moved in case of drought, storm, or cold.
- **Soil drainage risks**: Improper garden soil may lead to root rot.
- **Pest exposure**: Higher risk of insects, slugs, and soil pathogens.

Best practices for in-ground planting:

- Amend soil with **perlite, bark chips, and sand** for aeration and drainage.
- Plant in a **shaded or semi-shaded location** protected from heavy rain.
- Add mulch or leaf litter around the base (but not touching the stem) to retain moisture and mimic forest floor conditions.

If in doubt, opt for container growing until you're confident your outdoor environment can consistently support the plant's needs.

Outdoor cultivation of Christmas Cactus offers **rewarding opportunities for stronger growth, more vibrant blooming, and overall plant vitality**, especially when timed and executed with care. By understanding the species' tropical origins and mimicking those conditions, gardeners can extend their growing success beyond the windowsill.

Key takeaways for outdoor success include:

- Only place outdoors when **temperatures are reliably above 50°F.**
- Provide **filtered shade**, not direct sun.
- Transition the plant **gradually between environments**.
- Always return indoors before the **first sign of frost.**
- Choose **containers for control**, or plant in-ground only in **frost-free climates**.

With attention to detail and respect for seasonal shifts, your Christmas Cactus can transition from a houseplant to a garden treasure—one that blooms magnificently year after year.

DECORATIVE USES AND SEASONAL DISPLAY IDEAS

The Christmas Cactus is more than just a blooming houseplant—it's a symbol of tradition, a cherished holiday gift, and a decorative staple that brings natural beauty to winter festivities. As the days grow shorter and homes begin to sparkle with seasonal warmth, the vibrant, trailing blooms of Schlumbergera offer a stunning contrast to cold weather and bare landscapes.

Creative Holiday Display Arrangements

Christmas Cactus is uniquely suited for decorative display due to its cascading stems, bright blossoms, and compact growth. Unlike cut flowers, which fade within days, a blooming cactus can last for several weeks— making it ideal for holiday arrangements that require longevity, beauty, and ease of maintenance.

1. Living Holiday Centerpieces

A mature Christmas Cactus in full bloom is naturally eye-catching and can serve as a low-maintenance centerpiece.

133

- **Use a decorative ceramic pot** in seasonal colors like red, white, silver, or gold.
- Surround the base with small ornaments, pinecones, cinnamon sticks, or faux berries to add texture without interfering with watering.
- Place on a dining table, entryway, or kitchen island where it can be admired daily.
- For multi-plant centerpieces, combine with low-growing evergreens or succulents for visual contrast.

2. Window Display Setup

During the holiday season, windows become visual stages for décor seen from both inside and out. A brightly blooming Christmas Cactus adds color, life, and texture to windowsill arrangements.

- Pair with twinkle lights or battery-operated candles (placed at a safe distance).
- Use frosted window clings or faux snow sprays behind the cactus to create a festive backdrop.
- Avoid placing the plant directly against cold glass; instead, use a plant stand to elevate it slightly for air circulation.

3. Mantel and Shelf Displays

Mantels are classic spots for seasonal displays, and the arching stems of the cactus drape beautifully across edges.

- Position the pot slightly off-center and cascade stems downward toward one side for an organic effect.

134

- Integrate with garlands made of evergreen, eucalyptus, or fabric ribbon.
- Avoid placing the cactus near heat sources like fireplaces or space heaters.

4. Terrarium-Style Vignettes

Miniature Christmas Cactus plants or young cuttings can be displayed in glass terrariums with festive accents.

- Use wide-mouth jars, cloches, or shallow glass bowls with drainage layers.
- Decorate with holiday figurines, tiny LED lights, moss, or sand art.
- Provide indirect light and ventilation, as terrariums can become too humid if sealed.

5. Seasonal Entryways and Side Tables

Welcoming guests with a Christmas Cactus at the front door or in a foyer adds a touch of warmth and elegance.

- Place on a console table with a small chalkboard or wooden sign that reads "Merry & Bright" or "Season's Greetings."
- Add a miniature sleigh, lantern, or figurine nearby to complete the tableau.
- Avoid drafts from exterior doors that can stress the plant.

Each of these ideas uses the plant's natural aesthetic to anchor décor without requiring invasive modifications, ensuring both beauty and botanical health.

Hanging Baskets, Centerpieces, and Gift Ideas

The Christmas Cactus is a remarkably versatile plant that can adapt to a variety of containers and configurations, making it an excellent candidate for hanging displays, table arrangements, and thoughtful gifts.

1. Hanging Basket Arrangements

Because Christmas Cactus has a naturally arching, trailing growth habit, it thrives in hanging baskets—especially when placed where its blooms can dangle freely and catch the eye.

- Choose **woven or wire baskets** lined with coconut fiber or moss for a rustic look.
- Use **lightweight plastic pots** with drainage and suspend them using holiday-colored macramé hangers or gold/silver chains.
- Hang near windows with ample indirect light, ensuring no hot drafts or cold blasts from doors or vents.
- Consider incorporating ornaments or hanging decorations from the basket rim—just be sure they don't weigh down the plant.

2. Tabletop Centerpiece Styles

Small or medium Christmas Cactus plants can be transformed into stunning table accents:

- **Elevated Planter Style**: Place in a footed or pedestal planter to give height and prominence.

- **Cluster Style**: Group several small plants together, each in a unique pot, and unify with coordinated ribbon colors.
- **Wreath Accent Style**: Set a small plant at the center of a tabletop evergreen wreath for a "living candle" effect.

3. Gift-Wrapped Plant Presentation

Christmas Cactus makes a heartfelt, living gift for friends, family, and neighbors—especially when dressed for the season.

- Wrap the pot in **burlap, kraft paper, or seasonal fabric**, and secure with jute twine or festive ribbon.
- Include a hand-written **care card** with watering instructions and bloom tips.
- For an elegant touch, insert a small ornament or holiday tag into the soil.
- Use miniature pots of young propagated cactus as **stocking stuffers** or party favors.

4. "Blooming Basket" Gift Sets

Pair a blooming cactus with other holiday gifts in a basket for a holistic seasonal bundle.

- Add items like gourmet cocoa, holiday-scented candles, or handmade soaps.
- Choose a theme (e.g., "Warm Winter Wishes" or "Blooming Joy") and design the set around it.
- Include a small guide on plant care for recipients unfamiliar with succulents.

These decorative and gifting strategies add emotional warmth to the holidays while showcasing the beauty and resilience of Christmas Cactus.

Pairing with Other Winter Plants

To enhance your Christmas Cactus display or create a complete indoor winter garden, you can pair it with other plants that complement its shape, color, and seasonal flair. A well-curated combination adds dimension and interest without overshadowing the cactus's stunning blooms.

1. Holiday Plant Companions

- **Poinsettias** (*Euphorbia pulcherrima*): Their bold red bracts complement the cactus's more delicate blossoms.
- **Amaryllis**: Upright, trumpet-shaped blooms contrast beautifully with cascading cactus segments.
- **Cyclamen**: With ruffled petals and heart-shaped leaves, Cyclamen adds softness and winter color.
- **Norfolk Island Pine** (*Araucaria heterophylla*): A living mini-tree perfect for decorating alongside your cactus.
- **Paperwhite Narcissus**: Fragrant and graceful, they offer an elegant addition to tabletop arrangements.

2. Evergreen Accents

Use live evergreens to frame or support your Christmas Cactus display. Options include:

- Sprigs of **pine, fir, or cedar** woven into pot surrounds.

- Miniature potted **boxwood or rosemary trees** arranged in a tiered planter stand.
- Faux greenery garlands with embedded fairy lights for sparkle and structure.

3. Contrast with Leaf and Form

- Pair with **bold-leaf houseplants** like Chinese Evergreen (*Aglaonema*) or Peace Lily (*Spathiphyllum*) for lush texture.
- Add **trailing ivy or pothos** around the base of the cactus for a cascading effect.
- Use **succulent clusters** (e.g., Echeveria, Sedum) in small pots for a modern, minimal pairing.

4. Coordinated Containers

Group plants in containers of similar design, shape, or material for a unified appearance. For instance:

- All white ceramic pots for a snowy winter theme
- Rustic terra cotta pots for a farmhouse holiday look
- Metallic containers for glamorous, party-ready décor

With proper spacing and consideration of light and watering needs, these plant companions can turn a simple holiday cactus into a full living display that draws admiration from guests and family alike.

Seasonal Lighting and Decor Safety

Holiday décor often involves lights, candles, and decorative materials that can pose risks to houseplants. Knowing how to decorate **safely and responsibly** ensures your Christmas Cactus thrives throughout the season without stress or damage.

1. Light Placement Safety

- Use **LED lights** near your plant displays—they produce minimal heat compared to traditional bulbs.
- Avoid placing **string lights directly on the plant**, especially if they generate warmth.
- Never run electrical cords **under plant trays or across wet surfaces**.
- If displaying plants on mantels or shelves, **secure lights behind or above** the cactus—not in direct contact.

2. Ornaments and Decorative Picks

- Use **non-toxic materials** around your plants, especially if children or pets are present.
- Avoid placing sharp picks or glitter-laden ornaments in the soil, which can affect drainage or be accidentally ingested.
- When using decorative stones or moss, make sure they allow water to reach the roots.

3. Fire and Heat Hazards

- Never place your Christmas Cactus **near open flames**, such as candles or fireplaces.
- Keep the plant **away from heat vents**, radiators, or space heaters.
- Decorative candles near plant displays should be **battery-operated** or placed at a safe distance.

4. Stability and Tipping Prevention

- Ensure pots and containers are **well-balanced and stable**, especially in high-traffic areas.
- Use heavy bases or decorative planters with wide bottoms to avoid tipping.
- Secure hanging baskets properly to avoid dislodgement during holiday activities.

Decorating with a living plant requires mindfulness not only for aesthetics but also for **plant health and household safety**. Taking these precautions allows you to enjoy the season without unexpected damage to your displays or your cactus.

How to Keep It Looking Fresh for the Holidays

A blooming Christmas Cactus is stunning, but the challenge lies in **keeping it fresh, healthy, and vibrant** throughout the extended holiday season. Here are best practices to ensure your plant looks its best from December through January—and sometimes even into February.

1. Optimize Light and Temperature

- Place your cactus in a location with **bright, indirect light**—ideally near an east or north-facing window.
- Maintain temperatures between **60°F to 70°F (15°C to 21°C)** during the day, and slightly cooler at night.
- Avoid sudden temperature swings and keep away from heat vents and drafty windows.

141

2. Manage Watering Carefully

- Water only when the **top inch of soil is dry**, usually every 7–10 days in winter.
- Use **room temperature water** to avoid shocking the roots.
- Always empty excess water from saucers to prevent root rot.
- Mist occasionally if your home is very dry, especially near heating systems.

3. Support Bloom Longevity

- After buds appear, **don't move the plant frequently**—even small changes can cause buds to drop.
- Avoid overwatering once the plant is blooming.
- Deadhead spent flowers gently by pinching or snipping them off at the base.

4. Groom and Clean Regularly

- Remove dust or debris from the leaves with a soft brush or damp cloth.
- Trim damaged or faded segments using sterile scissors or pruning shears.
- Rotate the pot weekly for even light exposure and balanced growth.

5. Fertilizer During Blooming?

- During the bloom period, **hold off on fertilizing**—wait until the plant has finished flowering before resuming feeding.

- If using a bloom-boosting fertilizer in early fall, stop once buds are visible.

6. Address Signs of Stress Promptly

- **Buds falling off** may indicate temperature stress or overwatering.
- **Yellowing segments** can result from poor drainage or low humidity.
- Respond quickly by adjusting the environment—small tweaks often reverse symptoms.

With thoughtful placement and consistent care, your Christmas Cactus can remain the **jewel of your holiday display**—offering not only seasonal beauty, but a living celebration of patience, renewal, and tradition.

The Christmas Cactus brings something unique to the holiday season—a display that's alive, evolving, and bursting with natural beauty. Whether hanging from a festive basket, wrapped in ribbon as a gift, or glowing in the center of a holiday table, this plant is a celebration in and of itself.

By embracing its decorative potential, pairing it with other seasonal plants, and understanding how to display it safely and beautifully, you can create stunning holiday scenes that last well beyond the season. With a bit of creativity and a touch of care, your Christmas Cactus becomes more than a plant—it becomes a treasured part of your seasonal tradition.

CHAPTER SIX

FAQS AND ANSWERS FOR BEGINNERS

Every plant enthusiast—from novice growers to seasoned horticulturists—has questions about how to care for, maintain, and enjoy the Christmas Cactus to its fullest potential. Its unique bloom timing, epiphytic behavior, and delicate beauty make it both a delightful holiday companion and a plant that raises many queries.

This chapter answers the most common questions new owners ask when their cactus won't bloom, when it's ailing, or when they're unsure if it's safe to keep around pets. These clarifications will help readers make informed, confident decisions and form a deeper, more successful relationship with their Christmas Cactus.

Why Isn't My Christmas Cactus Blooming?

This is arguably the most common concern among new owners. When the winter holidays approach, many expect their Christmas Cactus to burst into festive bloom. But without certain environmental cues, the plant may stubbornly remain flowerless. Understanding this behavior begins with recognizing its **natural bloom cycle**.

1. The Role of Photoperiod and Temperature

The Christmas Cactus is **photoperiodic**, meaning it responds to light and darkness cues to initiate blooming. To trigger the flowering cycle, it requires:

- **12–14 hours of uninterrupted darkness** each night for approximately **6 weeks**.
- Nighttime temperatures ideally between **50°F to 55°F (10°C to 13°C)** during this period.

If your plant is exposed to artificial lighting at night (like from lamps, TVs, or streetlights), the bloom signal can be interrupted. Similarly, warm indoor temperatures that mimic summer conditions can confuse the plant into continuing vegetative growth rather than preparing to bloom.

2. Inadequate Rest Period

Another frequent mistake is failing to provide a **dormancy period** in the fall. Starting in September or early October, you should:

- **Reduce watering** to allow the soil to dry slightly between waterings.
- Stop fertilizing altogether.
- Move the plant to a cooler, darker space to begin the bloom trigger cycle.

Without this period of relative rest, your cactus may remain healthy but produce no buds.

3. Overfeeding or Excessive Growth

While feeding during the growth season is helpful, **too much nitrogen-rich fertilizer** can promote leafy segment growth at the expense of flowering. The plant gets the message to grow instead of bloom.

4. Bud Drop and Environmental Stress

Sometimes buds form but fall off before opening. This is usually caused by:

- Sudden changes in location, temperature, or humidity.
- Overwatering during the bud phase.
- Drafts or cold air.

Quick Blooming Checklist:

- Provide 12–14 hours of darkness nightly for 6 weeks.
- Keep night temperatures cool (50–55°F).
- Cut back on water and fertilizer during pre-bloom months.
- Avoid disturbing or moving the plant once buds appear.

When these conditions are met, the Christmas Cactus reliably rewards growers with cascades of jewel-toned flowers that last for weeks.

How Long Can They Live?

One of the most surprising and delightful facts about the Christmas Cactus is its **longevity**. Unlike many houseplants that fade after a few seasons, Christmas

Cacti are **remarkably long-lived** and often become **heirlooms passed from one generation to the next.**

1. Typical Lifespan

- In ideal conditions, a Christmas Cactus can **live 30 to 40 years** or more.
- Some specimens, particularly those propagated and handed down through families, are known to **exceed 75–100 years** in age.

2. Growth Stages Over Time

- **0–2 years**: A young plant will establish its root system, develop basic structure, and possibly produce its first sparse blooms.
- **3–5 years**: The cactus becomes more robust, with a dense stem structure and regular blooming.
- **5+ years**: Fully mature, with well-defined growth habits and significant blooming cycles.

3. Maintenance for Longevity

- **Regular repotting** every 3–4 years (or when root-bound).
- **Pruning and shaping** to maintain air circulation and growth direction.
- **Consistent seasonal care**, including bloom triggers and rest periods.

4. Cultural Value and Sentimental Importance

Many families treat the Christmas Cactus as more than just a plant—it becomes a symbol of tradition. It may sit in the same sunny kitchen window for decades, blooming on cue and delighting generations with its color. This emotional connection makes it a cherished houseplant unlike any other.

With care, a single plant can bloom for decades— becoming a witness to holiday memories year after year.

Can I Grow Them from Grocery Store Cuttings?

Absolutely—and in fact, this is a **wonderful way to start a new plant** or expand your collection. Many Christmas Cactus plants sold during the holidays are **affordable, pre-blooming specimens** in full color. Even if you find a cutting or small segment discarded or gifted, you can easily propagate it into a healthy new plant.

1. What You Need to Know Before You Begin

- **Schlumbergera** is highly responsive to vegetative propagation.
- You can propagate from **stem segments** (often just 2 or 3 segments long).
- It is important to **let cuttings callus** before placing them in soil or water to prevent rot.

2. How to Take and Plant a Grocery Store Cutting

- Choose a healthy, disease-free cutting with firm segments.
- Let the cut end air dry for **24–48 hours** until it forms a callus.

- Place it in **well-draining cactus mix** or a blend of peat and perlite.
- Keep the soil slightly moist but not soggy.
- In about 3–6 weeks, you'll see signs of new growth as roots establish.

3. Water Propagation Option

- You can also place callused cuttings in a **glass of clean water** (just deep enough to touch the base of the cutting).
- Once roots develop, transplant into soil.

4. Grocery Store Plant Concerns

Sometimes, these plants have been **force-bloomed** using chemicals or unnatural light cycles, which can leave them weak or confused. If you buy a bloomed plant:

- Let it **rest after flowering** by cutting back water and not fertilizing.
- **Re-pot** if the soil is compacted or water-retentive.
- Begin standard care to re-establish a healthy routine.

Growing from grocery store plants is rewarding, economical, and beginner-friendly. With patience, these inexpensive starts can become long-living members of your home.

Is It Safe Around Pets?

Pet owners are often rightly concerned about the safety of household plants, as many species can be toxic when ingested by curious cats and dogs. Fortunately, the

Christmas Cactus is **one of the safest houseplants to grow around pets.**

1. Toxicity Rating

According to multiple veterinary and horticultural sources, **Schlumbergera is non-toxic** to:

- Cats
- Dogs
- Horses
- Birds

This makes it a preferred holiday plant in homes with animals, unlike Poinsettias, Mistletoe, or Amaryllis, which are all toxic to pets if ingested.

2. What Happens If a Pet Eats It?

Although not toxic, **mild gastrointestinal upset** can occur if a pet eats a large quantity of the plant. Symptoms may include:

- Drooling
- Vomiting
- Diarrhea
- Loss of appetite (temporary)

These effects are typically mild and resolve on their own. If symptoms persist, consult a veterinarian.

3. Preventing Pet Interactions

- Place the cactus in **hanging baskets** or **elevated shelves** if your pet is particularly curious.
- For cats, placing citrus peels or natural deterrent sprays nearby can discourage nibbling.
- Secure pots to avoid tipping if pets rub against them or jump nearby.

4. Bird and Reptile Safety

If you keep birds or reptiles in the home, they too can safely coexist with the Christmas Cactus, provided it's kept out of enclosures and not sprayed with harmful pesticides or cleaners.

In short, the Christmas Cactus is a **safe, beautiful option for pet lovers** who don't want to compromise on holiday décor or houseplant joy.

What's the Easiest Way to Restart a Failing Plant?

Seeing a Christmas Cactus decline can be discouraging, but these plants are resilient and often bounce back if given the right care. If your cactus looks limp, shriveled, or fails to grow, don't give up—there's still time to revive it. Here's how to restart a struggling plant effectively.

1. Diagnose the Problem First

Common issues include:

- **Overwatering** (leading to root rot)
- **Underwatering** (leading to shriveled stems)

- **Poor light** (causing yellowing or elongated growth)
- **Old soil** (compacted, nutrient-depleted, or holding too much moisture)

2. Root Inspection

- Gently remove the plant from the pot and inspect the roots.
- **Healthy roots** are firm and white.
- **Rotted roots** are black, mushy, or foul-smelling—trim these away completely.

3. Emergency Re-Potting Protocol

- Clean the plant's base and let it air-dry for a few hours.
- Use **fresh, sterile cactus mix** with good drainage.
- Place in a **clean pot with drainage holes**.
- Water sparingly for the first two weeks—just enough to keep the soil barely moist.

4. Prune and Revive

- Remove severely damaged or rotting segments.
- Retain any healthy segments and repot them individually if necessary.
- Move the plant to a **bright, shaded area** and avoid direct sunlight during recovery.

5. Use Cuttings to Propagate If Necessary

If the plant is mostly dead but a few segments are healthy, you can **take cuttings** and start over.

- Follow standard propagation steps using soil or water.

- Begin a **fresh pot with new roots**, ensuring the best chance of survival.

6. Be Patient During Recovery

It can take **weeks to months** for a weakened plant to fully recover, especially if root damage was extensive. During this time:

- Maintain a consistent environment (light, temperature, humidity).
- Do not overwater.
- Avoid fertilizing until new growth appears.

7. Long-Term Outlook

A plant that has bounced back from distress often returns with **vigorous new growth and blooming** the following season. Reviving a failing Christmas Cactus is not just possible—it's deeply rewarding.

The Christmas Cactus is more than just a seasonal bloom or decorative plant. It is a **living metaphor for patience, resilience, and the joy of growth**—both botanical and personal. From its humble, unassuming green segments to the burst of unexpected color each holiday season, this plant rewards attentive care, curiosity, and observation over time. In a world that often demands instant gratification, growing a Christmas Cactus teaches something timeless: **great beauty takes time to prepare.**

Unlike fast-growing herbs or quickly fading annuals, the Christmas Cactus operates on its own gentle rhythm. It

invites us to slow down and tune into seasonal cycles—
shortening days, subtle temperature shifts, and
dormancy. In doing so, we begin to align with nature in
small, daily ways. We adjust the light, withhold water,
or shift the plant's position—not to control, but to
support.

This plant doesn't thrive under neglect, but neither does it
demand perfection. Instead, it calls for a middle ground
of **consistent attention and gentle correction**,
offering many second chances. If you forget to water, it
will likely forgive you. If you overwater, it may sulk—
but give it time, and it can bounce back. These are not
just gardening lessons. They are **life lessons**.

Moreover, the joy it brings is deeply emotional. The sight
of buds forming in November after months of
preparation can bring genuine excitement. The full
bloom near Christmas evokes a sense of seasonal
magic—especially when it returns each year, like an old
friend, dependable yet always wondrous.

As you close this book and begin your own Christmas
Cactus journey, remember this: **you are not just
growing a plant—you are cultivating awareness,
mindfulness, and a connection to something
greater.** Whether you're tending one pot or dozens,
sharing cuttings with friends, or passing down a plant
to the next generation, you're participating in a living
tradition.

Approach the process with patience. Celebrate each new
bud, each root, and every lesson learned from mistakes.

Let this resilient cactus brighten your windowsill, your holiday, and your heart for many years to come.

Quick-Start Plant Care Checklist

This cheat sheet summarizes everything you need to keep your Christmas Cactus thriving year-round. Use it as a go-to reference for routine care.

Basic Care

- **Light**: Bright, indirect light (east or north-facing window is ideal)
- **Temperature**: 60–70°F (15–21°C) during active growth; 50–55°F (10–13°C) to trigger blooming
- **Humidity**: Moderate to high; mist or use a humidity tray in dry climates
- **Watering**: Let soil dry about halfway before rewatering; water less in fall dormancy
- **Fertilizer**: Use balanced liquid fertilizer (10-10-10) monthly during spring and summer

Blooming Support

- **Dormancy Period**: 6 weeks in fall with cooler temperatures and long nights
- **Dark Cycle**: 12–14 hours of uninterrupted darkness nightly to set buds
- **Don't Move Plant**: Once buds form, avoid relocating the plant..

Potting

- **Soil**: Light, well-draining mix (cactus mix + perlite or orchid bark)
- **Repotting**: Every 3–4 years or when root-bound
- **Pot Type**: Clay or ceramic with drainage holes

Common Troubleshooting

- **Wilting** = Likely overwatering or poor drainage
- **No Blooms** = No dark cycle, too warm, or insufficient dormancy
- **Yellow Segments** = Overwatering, too much sun, or old soil
- **Falling Buds** = Environmental shock, drafts, or excessive movement

Glossary of Christmas Cactus Terms

Understanding the language of plant care helps simplify the learning process. Below are common terms you'll encounter when caring for a Christmas Cactus.

Adventitious Root
Roots that develop from non-root tissues, such as stem segments—common during propagation.

Bud Drop
The premature falling of flower buds, often due to stress such as movement, drafts, or inconsistent watering.

Callusing

The process where a plant wound dries and seals before rooting—critical when propagating cuttings.

Dormancy

A period of rest where growth slows, allowing energy to be stored for blooming. Triggered by cooler temperatures and shorter daylight.

Epiphyte

A plant that grows on another plant or object for support but is not parasitic. Schlumbergera are epiphytes in the wild.

Leaf Segment (Cladode)

Flattened stems resembling leaves. These are the plant's photosynthetic organs and form the structure of the Christmas Cactus.

Node

The point where segments join or where new growth and roots can emerge.

Overwatering

Too much moisture in the soil, often leading to root rot—a common problem in poorly-drained pots.

Photoperiodism

The response of a plant to the duration of light and darkness, influencing flowering in Christmas Cactus.

Root Bound

When roots outgrow the pot and circle around the inside, restricting water and nutrient uptake.

Schlumbergera
The genus name for Christmas Cactus and its relatives (including Thanksgiving and Easter Cactus).

Succulent
A plant adapted to storing water in leaves or stems. While the Christmas Cactus is not a desert cactus, it has succulent properties.

Transpiration
The release of water vapor from plant surfaces—affects humidity needs and hydration.

Well-Draining Soil
A mix that retains some moisture but allows excess water to flow freely to prevent root rot.

Seasonal Care Calendar

Use this calendar as your year-round roadmap for growing a thriving Christmas Cactus. While dates may shift depending on your climate, the plant's needs follow a natural annual rhythm.

Winter (December–February)
Focus: Blooming and gentle maintenance

- Enjoy flowers; do not move or repot while in bloom
- Lightly water when top inch of soil is dry
- Keep in bright, indirect light
- Remove faded blooms to encourage new ones

Spring (March–May)
Focus: Recovery and active growth

158

- Resume fertilizing once monthly (balanced 10-10-10)
- Begin watering regularly but don't allow soggy soil
- Prune to shape and encourage branching
- Repot if needed (after blooms fade and growth resumes)

Summer (June–August)
Focus: Robust growth and propagation

- Increase feeding to twice monthly during active growth
- Place outdoors in dappled light or shaded patio
- Monitor for pests like mealybugs and spider mites
- Start propagation from healthy cuttings
- Mist or increase humidity in dry climates

Fall (September–November)
Focus: Preparing for dormancy and blooming

- Reduce watering and stop fertilizing
- Move plant to a cool location with long nights
- Ensure at least 12–14 hours of darkness nightly
- Maintain temps between 50–55°F to trigger budding
- Avoid disturbing plant once buds form

Beginners often feel overwhelmed by a plant's needs or discouraged by small setbacks. But the Christmas Cactus, with its forgiving nature and festive flair, offers an excellent opportunity to learn, grow, and enjoy gardening success. By understanding its basic needs, responding to challenges with knowledge, and applying consistent care, even the most inexperienced plant parent can watch this beautiful cactus thrive year after year.

With its safe nature around pets, ease of propagation, and incredible lifespan, the Christmas Cactus isn't just a seasonal decoration—it's a companion for life.

The tools and templates in this appendix are designed to turn casual growers into confident caretakers. Whether you use them to track your first year or to reflect on decades of growing, they provide structure and insight into the rhythms of your plant's life. Your Christmas Cactus is not just a decoration; it's a dynamic, living part of your indoor garden—and with the knowledge and tracking provided here, you're well equipped to grow it with joy and long-term success.

THE END

Made in the USA
Monee, IL
17 December 2025